D0401740

FROM Motorcycle Consumer News

STREET STRATEGIES

A Survival Guide for Motorcyclists

BY David L. Hough

AUTHOR OF
Proficient Motorcycling

BOWTIE™ PRESS
Irvine, California

Ruth Strother, project manager
Nick Clemente, special consultant
Amy Fox, editor

Cover and book design copyright © 2001 by Michele Lanci-Altomare

Library of Congress Cataloging-in-Publication Data
Hough, David L., 1937-
Street strategies : a survival guide for motorcyclists / by David L.
Hough.
          p. cm.
Includes bibliographical references.
ISBN 1-889540-69-2 (Paperback with flaps : alk. paper)
1. Motorcycling-Anecdotes. 2. Motorcycling-Safety measures. I.
Title.
TL440.5 .H6723 2001
629.28'475--dc21
               2001003058

BowTie Press
A Division of Fancy Publications
3 Burroughs
Irvine, California 92618

Printed and bound in Singapore
10 9 8 7 6 5 4 3 2 1

Dedication

This book is dedicated to all you motorcycle safety instructors who have so generously given your time and energy both in the classroom and on the training range to help motorcyclists become more skilled and knowledgeable. Helping people avoid accidents isn't nearly as exciting as surgically putting hapless victims back together at the hospital, but training riders is a much better way to avoid pain—by helping motorcyclists avoid accidents in the first place.

—David L. Hough

Contents

Foreword — 7
Dedication — 9

Foreword

This book could save your life. How many books have you read that could make that statement?

As Editor of *Motorcycle Consumer News,* I receive a lot of reader mail intended for David Hough. We forward them to him sometimes dozens at a time.

Some are questions about riding gear or what roads to ride on an upcoming tour, which David always graciously answers in depth. Hough (pronounced "Huff") is a very well-rounded rider, a man who enjoys wrenching on his own motorcycles, a well-traveled two-wheeled world tourist, and a great storyteller around the campfire. You'd enjoy his company.

Other letters are from people who've suffered an accident and are asking what they might have done differently. These are tough, but David always does his best to help them come to terms with the event, learn the lesson, and to move on.

But our favorite letters are the grateful real-life stories of how one of David's riding tips has just accomplished its intended purpose and prevented an accident.

I can't image a greater satisfaction than to receive a letter from someone who credits you with saving his/her life. So I can understand why David has dedicated so much of his life to this work. It certainly wasn't for financial gain, as the time and effort involved could have been spent much more profitably on many other projects.

Personally, I think he's been inspired by the camaraderie we feel as motorcyclists—that special bond between otherwise very different people who are all involved in a sport that relatively few know and appreciate. And I think it's this sense of fellowship that motives his selfless acts of rider education.

Read these stories and commit their lessons to memory. "Be prepared," as the Boy Scouts say. Don't dwell on calamity, but be alert and focused and enjoy your ride. There's a lifetime of thoughtful riding wisdom in these pages, any tidbit of which might one day be crucial.

All of us at *Motorcycle Consumer News* are very proud of our long association with David's work and of being the monthly magazine that brought these pages to first light.

Best wishes for a safe and memorable ride.

– Dave Searle

Editor

Motorcycle Consumer News

Introduction

I started writing "Street Strategies" back in the 1970s when I was commuting to work at Boeing by motorcycle through Seattle traffic. In those days—before the big boom in motorcycling—very little information about riding skills was available. My brainstorming goal was to write riding tips that were brief enough to be read on the spot, rather than stuffed in a saddlebag and forgotten. I volunteered to be the Safety Coordinator for the Boeing Employees' Motorcycle Club (BEMC), and started generating these skill tips to hand out at the monthly club meetings. In addition, I usually carried a supply of my latest tips to offer to other motorcyclists with whom I fraternized while commuting to work.

Some of these tips came to the attention of the Washington Department of Licensing, who offered to hand them out at drivers' licensing offices.

The "Street Strategies" concept was redefined in the early 1980s, when the Motorcycle Safety Foundation (MSF) discovered some of these old BEMC skill tips, and asked me to write a series specifically for them. I agreed, in hopes that the MSF might publish and distribute a monthly "Street Strategy" series to motorcycle publications, organizations, dealer showrooms, and drivers' licensing departments, as a free service and a plug for the MSF.

After submitting a hefty package of forty tips to the MSF, I waited to see the results. Time passed. It wasn't until several years later, when the MSF created the Experienced RiderCourse, in which they published shortened versions of a few of my tips in the back of the *Instructor Guide,* that I got to see my work being used across America, even though it was only one-fourth of the tips I had written.

In the early 1980s, I expanded some of the tips into articles and started contributing them to *Road Rider* magazine, which later became *Motorcycle Consumer News (MCN).* Those simple one-page street-riding tips grew into articles for a long-running monthly column, "Proficient Motorcycling" (which still runs today and was assembled into a comprehensive book, *Proficient Motorcycling,* in 2000).

Despite the success of "Proficient Motorcycling," I noticed that motorcyclists still seem to appreciate the shorter versions that can be read on their morning work breaks or while waiting for their club breakfasts to begin. Even twenty-five years after I first began writing the articles, *MCN* continues to receive letters from readers who recall one or more of the brief tip sheets that started a lifelong interest in riding skills or helped them avoid what could have been a nasty accident.

When Fred Rau became an editor of *MCN* in 1992, he began including the "Street Strategy" tips from the MSF *Instructor Guide*, with their permission as a column. At the time, I was enthused that a national publication was finally making good use of them, but by the end of 1994, Fred had published all of them. It seemed like it would be a good April Fools' Day joke on the MSF staff for *MCN* to come up with an additional "Street Strategy" as a parody of the style that the MSF had used in their Instructor Guide. I knew most of the MSF staff, and knew that they read *MCN*, but I also suspected that few would remember where "Street Strategies" had come from. I could just imagine them spotting the rogue "Street Strategy" in *MCN*, and furiously flipping through their old *Instructor Guides* looking for it. To add to the joke, I requested that Fred not add any byline.

The joke fell on its face when the rogue "Street Strategy" parody missed the April issue and slid into May. Then a couple of months later, the MSF fell into a budget crunch and most of the employees—at least the few who knew the history of "Street Strategies"—were laid off. So much for the famous 1995 April Fools' joke. Ironically, however, Fred didn't see the rogue "Street Strategy" as a parody. He felt it filled a need, and asked me to write some more. So I continued writing them from 1995 until the Spring of 2000 when I missed a deadline because of an extensive trip.

The next time Fred and I saw each other was at the Americade motorcycle rally in New York. At that time he confided that "Street Strategies" was using up valuable space, and since no one had ever commented on the series, it was time to discontinue it and use the space for something more important. I agreed, happy to be relieved of a responsibility. After all, a couple of the "Street Strategies" had been repeated by mistake, and the normally sharp-eyed readers hadn't noticed, and no one had complained about the issues that didn't include a "Street Strategy."

But the very next month after our mutual decision, the latest *MCN* Reader Survey shocked us with the news that "Street Strategies" was high on readers' priorities. Fred sent me a frantic e-mail, and I furiously cranked out some additional strategies to make the publishing deadline.

So, maybe we've come full circle. Although many motorcyclists request a detailed four-page explanation of some riding tactic, complete with vector diagrams and photographs, others seem to appreciate brief, spontaneous tips that can be absorbed in a couple of minutes.

This book isn't organized by topic. Each tip stands alone. However, before you dive in, be aware that most of these tips involve an accident or near miss. You can get pretty paranoid reading these tips one after another. Be aware that no one person is likely to encounter the whole shebang in a lifetime of riding. Flip through the pages whenever you have a spare moment, and read whatever strikes your fancy. Perhaps one of these "Street Strategies" will help you keep the shiny side up when you stumble into a similar situation.

Alley Alert

Don't Let Your Guard Down Between Intersections

You're riding down a quiet residential street. Traffic is light, the road surface is clean, and you have a clear view of the street ahead. Approaching an intersection where the view is partially blocked by tall hedges, you cover the front brake and scrutinize the side streets for cross-traffic, bicyclists, and pedestrians. The intersection is clear, so you roll back on the throttle and continue on your relaxed ride.

But right in the middle of the next block, a car suddenly darts out of an alley hidden between two garages. You reach for the front brake and squeeze the lever as hard as you can just short of skidding the tire, but even your best quick-stop technique can't bring the bike to a halt short of a collision. Your front wheel crumples into the left car door as the startled driver slams on his brakes.

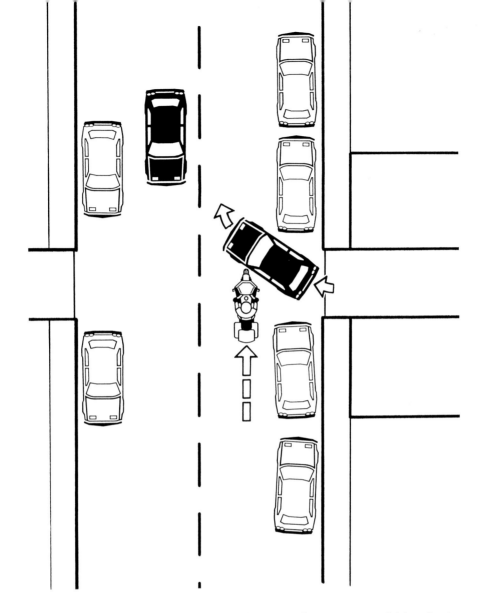

You already know that intersections are dangerous, and it's wise to cover the front brake in the event a quick stop is needed. But we tend to forget that alleys also intersect the street, and most alleys are so narrow that the view of emerging traffic is limited. As a measure of our complacency, statistics show that 13 percent of all motorcycle accidents occur at alleyways or driveways, yet they account for 17 percent of motorcycle fatalities.

You should be just as cautious approaching the alley as when you cross a busy intersection. Slowing from 40 to 30 mph will cut your stopping distance in half. You also can move to a lane position that offers a better view of the situation. And your reaction time will be much shorter if you are already covering the front brake lever.

14 Arrow Slides

Some of Those White Arrows on the Surface Are As Slick As Ice

You have just turned off the superslab, and the curving off-ramp leads down to an intersection. There, the traffic signal is red so you apply the brakes gently while leaned over in the curve, then brake harder as the motorcycle straightens up.

Suddenly, the front tire loses traction and begins to slide sideways. You release the front brake to regain balance and prevent a spill, and just as suddenly the rear tire fishtails. You stay on the rear brake to prevent a high-side flip, thereby keeping the motorcycle upright, but you only manage to bring the machine to a stop with the front wheel out in the traffic lane. Fortunately, other drivers see you and swerve to avoid a collision.

Next time it would be a good idea to observe the white directional arrow glued to the pavement. Such directional markings are often made of a durable yet slick white plastic that can be especially treacherous when coated with oil drippings or rainwater. Select a path of travel to one side of the arrow, or if you can't avoid crossing the slick surface, you can brake harder in a straight line before your tires reach the problem area, then ease off the brakes to conserve traction.

16 Backing Bashers

It Shouldn't Be a Surprise When a Car Backs Out of a Parking Space

You've made a quick trip to the store to buy some plastic ties. With your purchase safely stowed in a saddlebag, you remove the disc lock, strap on your helmet, zip up your jacket, slip on your gloves, and start the engine. You're anxious to get home and continue a wiring project. With a quick look around, you snick up the sidestand and accelerate away from your parking spot.

Riding down the lane between the rows of parked cars, you watch for stray shopping carts, children darting between cars, and other drivers turning into the lane the wrong way. The lane is clear except for a man loading some bags into the trunk of a car ahead on your right. When he goes around to the passenger side, you assume he is still loading, and not about to drive away.

The instant the passenger door closes, however, the car is already backing out into your path. You reach for the front brake lever and attempt to make a quick stop, but the car backs out so quickly that you can't stop short of slamming your front tire into the car's bumper. It's a minor collision, but now you're confronted by two angry men who claim it was your fault. Apparently, there was a driver in the car, just waiting for the passenger to get in. Since you couldn't see the driver, he couldn't see you either.

Any vehicle with people getting in or out should be suspect of possible sudden movement. You should keep your attention focused on the action around a car, rather than allowing your mind to wander to what you are going to do later. If you slow down, you can give yourself more time to react to whatever might happen. And you will be better prepared for a quick stop if you cover the clutch and front brake levers.

One More Reason to Stay Out of the Center of the Lane

You're riding home from work in big-city rush hour traffic. Everyone seems to be creeping along, and when traffic does start to move, every signal seems to turn red just in time to hold up the car ahead of you. You're concerned about the engine overheating and anxious to get moving. It's frustrating waiting for the lights to turn green, and you pull up right behind the car ahead as if to urge the driver to get moving as soon as the light turns green.

You can see the reflection of the amber light for the cross street, so you know when it is time to snick into gear and be ready to move. As the signal turns green, the car ahead begins to move, and you accelerate right behind it, not wasting any time.

But a second later the front wheel suddenly dives downward, the bike comes to a sudden stop, and you are flung over the handlebars. Amid a screeching of tires, you slam onto the pavement and slide to a stop on your stomach in the middle of the intersection, wondering what happened.

What happened was that a temporary steel plate over a construction hole had slid sideways far enough to expose a gap at one side, just wide enough to swallow your front wheel. The car wheels bridged the hole, but your front wheel fell into it, bringing the bike to an instant stop. You didn't notice the construction plate because you had stopped so close to the car ahead that you couldn't see the road surface ahead. Furthermore, you were so intent on moving that you failed to monitor the surface when traffic started to move.

When stopping in traffic, it is always smart to leave a space cushion of at least a bike length between you and the vehicle ahead, both to provide a better view of the situation and to make yourself more visible. Also, it is a good idea to favor the left wheel track of autos ahead of you to avoid debris, spilled oil, and greasy paving.

20 Blinding Lights

Focus on the Fog Line to Protect Your Night Vision

You're on your way home from a weekend trip, during which you traveled a little farther than you had intended. Sunday evening traffic is heavy, and the setting sun is making it difficult to see. You realize it's going to turn into a nighttime ride so you stop for a break. At a nearby gas station, you gas up the bike, make a quick check of your lights, and head for a restaurant. While waiting for your meal, you swap your tinted faceshield for the clear shield you carry and wash it clean with some soap and water in the bathroom so you won't have to waste any time getting back on the road.

After dinner, you quickly put on your gear and continue your ride home. But the blacktopped road is awfully difficult to see, and every time a car approaches from the opposite direction, it seems to take several seconds for your eyes to recover from the bright headlights. Just as you lean over into a sweeping left-hander, an oncoming car with misadjusted lights blinds you. When you finally begin to regain your vision, you realize you're headed off onto the shoulder. Barely are you able to maintain control in the loose gravel and get the bike pointed back onto the pavement again. It could have been a nasty crash.

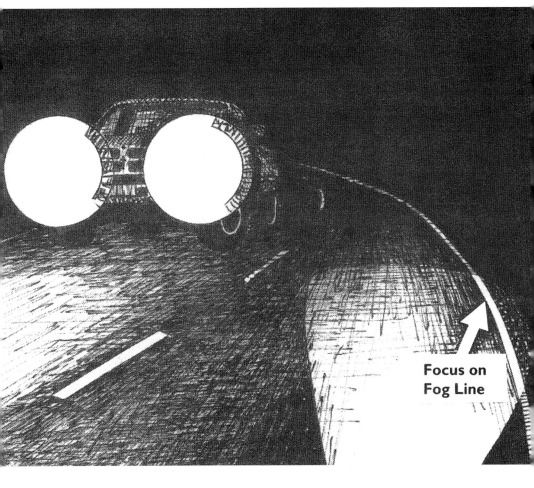

Focus on Fog Line

If your daytime ride is moving into the night, it's a good idea to change your dark-tinted face shield for a clear one and to check your lights. But you must realize that it takes several minutes for your eyes to adapt to darkness after being exposed to bright lights. When leaving a building at night you should pause in the dark for a few minutes before continuing the ride to allow time for your eyes to adjust from the bright indoor lights to the darkness, or you can wear your sunglasses inside at night.

When you're blinded by the glare of headlights, it takes several seconds for your eyes to adjust. One trick veteran motorcyclists use at night is to focus on the white fog line at the edge of the road as an oncoming vehicle passes. That way, your central vision doesn't get blinded, and after the vehicle has passed, you can return your focus to the road ahead.

Blind-Spot Blunders

Does the Truck Driver in the Next Lane See You?

Traffic is bumper-to-bumper on the freeway this afternoon, so you're riding on full alert. You try to leave enough following distance to avoid running into the car ahead of you or getting hit from behind. It's frustrating and potentially dangerous to be squeezed in between larger vehicles as traffic moves a few feet then stops. Eventually, you realize that the right lane of the freeway is closed for repairs, and everyone must merge into the left lane.

Most of the drivers ahead are politely allowing alternate vehicles to merge, so you plan to do the same. But there are four trucks next to you, and you realize the third truck is signaling and starting to move left. You ease into the left-wheel track, then slow to give yourself more space.

But as the truck moves over, you see that the moving van behind it is also moving, right on top of you. You swerve over the line onto the narrow shoulder to avoid getting crushed, accelerate up alongside the cab, and beep your horn. The errant moving-van driver finally sees you, but there is nothing he can do now except shrug his shoulders and allow you to squeeze in between him and the other truck.

Motorcyclists must accept the fact that bikes are small and, therefore, difficult to see in traffic. It's especially difficult for truck drivers to see a motorcycle in their mirrors. A driver of a large moving van may be looking in his or her mirror to determine whether there is space to merge and not see a motorcycle hidden in the blind spot.

However, you have more options than just continuing to creep along in traffic, allowing yourself to get into a merging blunder. You can move up alongside the cab of a truck to be seen better or you can move over to the right lane behind a car, so that when you merge back into the left lane you will be in a better position. Yes, you may lose your place in line, but that's better than losing your life.

Blind Spotters

Riding in the Blind Spots of Cars Is an Invitation to a Collision

You're out for a little spin on a warm summer evening. The big V-twin is throbbing along in the lights of the boulevard, and you're really enjoying the ride, even though there are more motorists on the street than you would prefer. You pretend not to see heads turning to admire your custom cruiser as you ride on by, but it's satisfying to know that your hours of polishing and painting have not gone unnoticed.

But approaching the entrance to a shopping mall, the driver of a car on your left suddenly swerves over into your lane, almost on top of you, brakes, and begins to turn into the mall parking lot, without signaling. Panicked, you beep your horn and try to steer out of the way. It takes the driver several seconds to wake up and realize he's almost on top of a motorcycle. He jams on the brakes, but it's too late. The bike low sides and jams under the side of the car. You manage to roll off and avoid serious injury, but your custom paint job is ruined, and you are furious at the driver's inattention.

While it's fun to cruise, it's important to maintain your awareness of other vehicles. And even a shiny custom motorcycle can be hard to spot in nighttime traffic. The other driver may be the one who makes a mistake, but you can contribute to accident by riding in the right rear blind spot of another vehicle. Riding in another driver's blind spot is an invitation to a collision. And even if it isn't your fault, it's your bike that gets crunched.

Bouncing Boards

Don't Be Surprised by Loose Planks at Railroad Crossings

You're riding through an industrial section of the city. The two-lane street has a number of railroad sidings with bumpy wooden planks next to the rails, but since the tracks cross the street at almost right angles, you aren't especially concerned about losing traction.

As you're about to cross the final siding, you see a heavily loaded 18-wheeler approaching from the opposite direction and calculate that the truck will cross the rails at just about the same time as your bike. You momentarily wonder why you bothered to observe this meaningless detail, and choose to maintain your speed and lane position.

But as you get closer to crossing the tracks, something causes you to change your mind. You decelerate slightly, so that you won't be crossing the tracks at the same instant as the truck, and you move toward the outside of your lane to allow the truck more room.

When the heavy truck bounces over the tracks, you're shocked to see one of the large planks bounce a foot in the air on your side of the centerline. Apparently, the plank next to the rail was loose, and the weight of the truck was sufficient to bounce the other end into the air. Because you changed speed and position, you saved yourself from what could have been a nasty accident.

Sometimes, you may not recognize the exact potential hazard in a situation, but something causes you to take evasive action anyway. The details that your brain picks up are not meaningless but are clues based on memories of other potentially hazardous situations. Paying attention to small details often makes the difference between an accident and a close call.

28 Bounding Bambis

In Deer Country, a Smart Rider Is Prepared for a Quick Stop

You're out for an early ride in the country, away from the hassles of traffic. The narrow backroad on which you travel passes farms and curves through a shady forest. You're aware of the hazards of backroads, such as loose gravel and wet leaves, so for this ride you're wearing your most protective riding gear: leathers, gloves, and full-coverage helmet. And you plan to keep the gear on even when the sun begins to warm the air.

You settle into a comfortably aggressive ride, slowing only for locations where there are narrow bridges and many hidden driveways. When you enter a deer migration area, you maintain speed, but watch carefully for wild deer alongside the road.

Suddenly, as you round a tight turn, you see a brown shape in the left ditch—perhaps a log or a soggy cardboard box. But a second later, the brown shape raises its head, and you instantly recognize the tall ears of a deer. But the deer just continues to stand there munching, so you assume you can cruise by without any evasive action.

But a second or two before you pass, the deer springs into action, scrambling onto the pavement directly in front of you. You attempt to brake and swerve, but the deer darts one way and then the other, and you can't avoid a collision that knocks both you and the deer to the pavement. Fortunately, neither of you is seriously hurt. The deer clatters away, leaving you to survey the damage to your bike. You silently congratulate yourself for wearing your leathers today.

DEER MIGRATION
NEXT 14 MILES

NIGHT
45

The reason for deer signs is that there is a history of numerous deer strikes in that area. So when you enter a deer zone, you should expect to encounter wild deer grazing alongside or leaping across the road. Deer typically spring into action as a vehicle gets close. The best tactic for avoiding a deer strike is to be prepared for a quick stop. If you see a deer next to the road you should immediately brake, especially if the deer is facing the road and, therefore, most likely to leap in your direction.

Bucking Bumps

An Angled Pavement Edge Can Throw You out of the Saddle

You're finally heading out for a weekend ride, glad to be on the road, away from responsibilities. The weather is perfect, the bike is running great, and you're looking forward to a two-day trip to clear your head. You've ridden this highway frequently and know its tricks and turns, so you can focus on the ride.

A few miles out of town you're surprised to see dust ahead, since this is a paved highway. You wonder if there has been an accident. But as you round a corner you see some construction signs and realize a section of road is being repaved. You slow down, and when you see a Bump sign, you prepare to absorb the impact by rising slightly on the footpegs.

However, just as you're about to bounce over the edge of the pavement, you see the edge is cut away at an angle rather than straight across the lane, with loose gravel on one side. As your front wheel drops into the gravel, it plows back toward the edge of the pavement, and you begin to lose balance. The bike crashes over on its side. It's not a serious accident, but you presumed you could handle a little gravel.

You should realize that a Bump sign means a difference in level between two surfaces, even if the edge is at an angle rather than straight across the lane. When you see construction signs, you should observe the road surface carefully, noticing if there is an angled pavement edge. An angled edge of pavement can trap your bike's front tire and prevent you from countersteering to maintain balance. To successfully negotiate such edge traps you must cross at more of an angle to prevent your front wheel from getting trapped by the edge.

Bumper Bikes

It Pays to Cover That Front Brake in Traffic

You're headed home from a Sunday ride. Traffic's heavy, and moving fast. You're overheated and tired from a long day, but you have to maintain a fast pace on the superslab to keep from getting pushed aside by aggressive drivers.

When you finally get to your turnoff, you breathe a sigh of relief for having survived the insane rush of Sunday afternoon freeway traffic and continue homeward on the busy four-lane arterial. You try to maintain at least a two-second following distance, but other drivers zoom into your space, and you react by closing up the distance and covering the brake lever. You can only hope no one does anything stupid.

You know you'll be getting home later than planned, and you glance down at the clock for a second. When you look up again, the car ahead of you has its brake lights on. You brake as quickly as you can, but there just isn't space to get the bike stopped, short of a collision. Your front wheel bangs into the vehicle ahead, and the car behind you squeals to a stop with its bumper crunching your saddlebags. You aren't hurt, but your bike will need some repairs, and you now have an accident to deal with.

Even if you're almost home, it is more important to maintain your guard on surface streets than it is on aggressive freeways. Thinking about your late arrival and glancing at the clock can distract you from what is happening ahead. Covering the brake lever is a good tactic, but it takes more than hope to avoid collisions in bumper-to-bumper traffic.

In heavy traffic, you should look ahead several vehicles to monitor traffic flow and signal lights to predict a traffic slowdown well before the brake lights of the next vehicle come on. You also could favor the left wheel track of the car ahead of you to make it easier to see and be seen. When you notice a slowdown ahead, apply your brakes to signal drivers behind you, which might prevent a chain of accidents.

Bus Blammers

Clever Riders Don't Hide Behind Busses in Traffic

You're a veteran motorcyclist, but almost all of your riding has been just for fun. Now, with commuter traffic clogging up the highways, you've started to use the motorcycle for the daily commute. Suddenly, you're spending most of your riding time in traffic rather than on the backroads or on cross-country trips. This morning you're following the same familiar route, which includes several miles of a heavily traveled arterial. When you see the front wheel of a bus at the curb suddenly turn in your direction, you roll off the gas and brake lightly to avoid a collision. But now you're riding directly behind the bus with a limited view of the street ahead.

Approaching a major intersection, you decide to stay behind the bus rather than attempt to change lanes. But before the bus can clear the intersection, you're surprised by a car making a left turn immediately behind the bus. You swerve toward the right and narrowly avoid getting hit by the left-turner, and then swerve back into the lane. But it's a close call that could have been deadly.

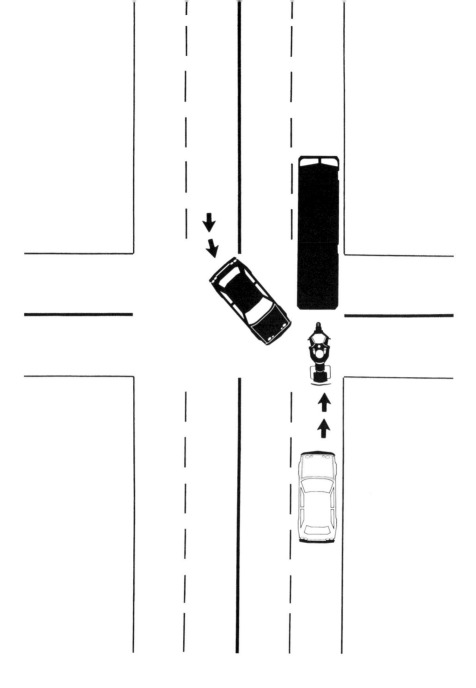

In some states, busses have the right-of-way even when pulling out from a bus stop. It is right to yield to a bus, but you should never follow immediately behind busses, trucks, or other large vehicles where you're hidden from the view of oncoming drivers. Rather than follow immediately behind a bus, you should change lanes or at least drop back to open up the view. Once you know from experience which lanes are used by transit busses, it's wise to avoid those lanes.

Center Strikes

36

Remember That Loose Debris Gets Pushed to the Center of the Lane

You're riding in heavy traffic with your defenses on full alert. All three lanes are crowded with cars, and you're especially attentive to vehicles around you that might suddenly change lanes or stop. You maximize your road space by riding in the center of your lane. To discourage another driver from suddenly changing lanes right in front of you, you close up the gap, but you compensate for the too-close following distance by looking over and around the vehicles ahead to spot hazards, and cover the clutch and front brake lever.

Suddenly, a large brick appears from under the car ahead, exactly in the center of the lane. Before you can even think about swerving, the bike's front wheel is vaulted upward, then the rear end is thrown sideways as the rear tire also ricochets off the spinning brick. You barely manage to avoid a spill, but the bike is now wobbling. Working your way to the side of the road, you discover that both rims are severely dented and the tires are going flat.

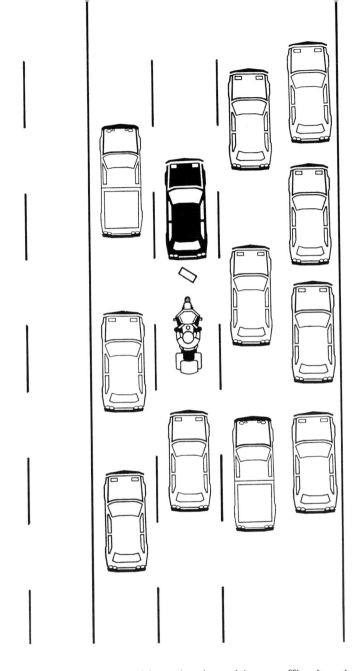

Sometimes you can't avoid getting boxed into traffic situations that don't allow an adequate view of the road surface. While it is wise to scrutinize traffic ahead and prepare for a quick stop, riding in the center of the lane exposes you to surface hazards such as wooden blocks, potholes, pavement breaks, grease strips, or bricks, which four-wheeled vehicles can straddle. When the close proximity of traffic prevents you from having an adequate view of the street surface ahead, you might consider riding in one of the wheel tracks rather than the center of the lane.

Running Wide Is a Clue Your Cornering Skills Need an Upgrade

It's Saturday—a great day for a ride with your friends. You've headed out in a group to "strafe some canyons," and you're confident your new machine has enough power to you to keep up with your companions. You don't want to be seen as a slow rider. The other guys are pushing fast, however, and you have to struggle to keep up, accelerating hard in the short straights and riding the brakes deep into the tight corners. When your tires twitch nervously in the tighter turns, you're convinced that you're riding about as fast as you can, yet the others are leaving you behind.

Halfway around a tight right-hander, the bike seems to have a mind of its own, refusing to turn as tightly as it should. You're trying to stay in the middle of your lane, but the front wheel drifts across the centerline. You instinctively roll the throttle closed and apply the brakes. The bike seems to squat and drift even wider, and you can't avoid running off the pavement into a field. Luckily, there wasn't a car coming around the corner at that moment.

Crossing the centerline may seem to be a result of riding quickly, but the real culprit is your cornering technique. Use the whole lane—not just the center—to maximize traction. Approaching a right-handed turn, get the bike way over toward the centerline, use both brakes to decelerate, then get off the brakes before you lean over. Swivel your head around toward the direction you want to go, push on the right grip to lean right, and roll on a little throttle to pull the machine around the curve. Consider practicing your cornering techniques by yourself before joining the next group ride.

Desperate Drivers

Some Drivers Hate Motorcycles—Others Are Just Mentally Unstable

Riding along a secondary highway, you come up on a problem driver. He wanders from one side of the lane to the other, brakes to a crawl in corners, then exceeds the speed limit in the straights where passing him should have been possible. As other vehicles begin to collect behind you, you decide to get serious about passing to separate yourself from a potentially dangerous situation.

With a clear straight coming up, you signal, accelerate, check your mirror, and pull out to pass. When the problem driver sees your attempt to pass, he tries to speed up, but your bike has the acceleration advantage, and you quickly get by, signal, and pull back in line ahead of him. You're surprised to see the driver roar up close behind you, beeping his horn and shaking his fist. You accelerate quickly to avoid a rear-end collision, and open up some space by riding well over the speed limit.

If you haven't encountered a desperate driver yet, you will. And whatever his or her problem is, you don't want any part of it. Erratic driving, and even the condition of the vehicle itself, are clues that a driver has a problem, whether physical or psychological. You should understand that passing someone else can be interpreted by some as an act of aggression, especially if you tailgate, pass aggressively, or pull back in line too closely. Other drivers can interpret a normal pass as a challenge or an affront. And remember that some people are prejudiced against motorcyclists.

If you find yourself in this situation, separate yourself from a potential problem by increasing your distance from the other vehicle, both prior to the pass and when pulling back in line. You also have other options, such as pulling over for a break or turning off onto an alternate route.

Detour Dumping

Sooner or Later, You'll Find Yourself Riding Off Pavement

You've had a great road trip so far, and it's only another hundred miles from home when you see brake lights in the distance, and then suddenly a big orange sign: Pavement Ends. You can't believe it. You're on a paved state highway, but apparently the whole road has been torn up for construction during tourist season! You've got no choice but to struggle through the detour on a bike loaded with gear. As you bounce off the pavement, you realize the detour surface is rutted sand, slippery mud, and loose gravel.

Your front tire sinks in the ruts and the steering gets sluggish. Instinctively, you slow down and drag your feet to help stabilize the bike, but it wobbles even more, and when the front tire plows into a deep patch of gravel, you can't keep it upright. You aren't hurt, but there are now gravel scratches on your shiny roadburner, and you're both angry at the construction zone and embarrassed at not being able to get through without falling.

When faced with a deep patch of gravel, increase your speed to build forward energy. Then select the most tractable surface, such as the hard-packed dirt between the ruts or one side of the deep gravel. Rather than slowing to a crawl and extending your feet, place most of your weight on the footpegs and keep your speed up. Standing on the pegs places your weight down low on the machine, which allows you better control of your balance. Rolling on more throttle helps push the front tire through loose dirt and gravel, and helps steer the bike.

Sooner or later, all of us encounter road detours or repaving operations where we have no choice but to ride off pavement, and that requires different skills. If loose or slippery surfaces make you nervous, it's a good idea to learn some "dirt" riding skills before you encounter your next detour in traffic.

Double Trouble

A Second Left-Turner Can Be Worse Than the First

You've been using the bike more and more to commute to work because it saves time and frustration. Commuting in traffic has provided you with a lot of reminders to watch for: jaywalking pedestrians, drivers running red lights, and trucks swerving partially into your lane. You are especially aware of left-turning cars at intersections. This afternoon you're on your way home, riding a four-lane arterial. Traffic is lighter than normal, so you're able to ride a little faster than the posted limit.

Approaching an intersection, you observe a sport utility vehicle (SUV) facing the opposite direction about to turn left. You have the green light, but you predict the driver might turn left in front of you anyway, so you roll off the gas and move left to give yourself more room. Sure enough, the SUV driver does turn left in front of you, and you get back on the gas to continue through the intersection, silently complimenting yourself on your traffic skills.

But suddenly the van that was behind the SUV in the left turn lane begins to accelerate and turn. You quickly roll off the throttle and reach for the front brake lever as the van driver suddenly sees you, panics, and jams on the brakes. You're still braking as hard as you can when your front wheel thuds into the side of the van and you're thrown over the top.

When you are watching for left-turners, it's smart to be prepared in case they decide to turn in front of you and to move over to give yourself more room in case they do, but you should predict that a second driver might also attempt a quick left turn. Yes, that van driver in this scenario was at fault. Such a driver may not see you, or not realize you are approaching as quickly as you are. But all in all, you're the one who gets injured if he or she hits you.

Remember that riding at a faster speed makes it more difficult for other drivers to judge your approach speed and also increases your stopping distance. You should be in the habit of squeezing the front brake lever lightly when approaching intersections to reduce reaction time and dry the discs. Even if you have the green light, you should be squeezing the front brake to slow down and be prepared for a possible quick stop.

Those Steep Edges of New Pavement Can Be Your Downfall

You're on a quiet two-lane highway in forest country, enjoying a relaxed July ride. There are signs that deer are present, so you continue to watch the sides of the road. You also know that logging trucks come roaring through, so you check your mirrors occasionally. And when you do see an empty logging truck gaining on you rapidly, you move over into a convenient slower-traffic lane to let the trucker by. Suddenly your tires bump down over a steep pavement edge, and you realize the left lane has just been repaved. At the end of that lane, you gradually ease back toward the left, but when your front wheel hits the edge of the new pavement, the handlebars are suddenly yanked from your grasp, and the bike slams over onto its left side in a shower of broken plastic.

Fortunately, your decision to wear your leathers today paid off in limiting your injuries to bruises, and the bike is still operable, but you can't believe how quickly you lost control of balance.

SLOWER TRAFFIC KEEP RIGHT

While it is wise to let faster moving traffic go by, you should be more aware of the road surface before changing lanes. Even though there may not be any warning signs of an edge trap, the difference in color and texture of the new and old paving is a clue. You should expect hazardous edge traps wherever highway repaving is in progress. Steep pavement edges can trap the front tire of a two-wheeler and make it very difficult to maintain balance if you approach at a narrow angle. To bounce the front wheel up and over such edge traps without falling, it is essential to move away from the edge and then swing back at a wider angle—preferably at least 45 degrees.

A Raised Pavement Edge Is a Special Hazard to Two-Wheelers

You're on your way home from a rally, riding your big touring bike on a crowded two-lane highway. Sunday traffic has been congested, and you're getting frustrated with the slow progress. Now traffic as far ahead as you can see has come to a complete stop in a construction zone. You start thinking about passing the cars a few at a time, and moving up to the front of the line. There isn't much room at the left side of the new paving, but there are long periods of time when opposing traffic is apparently being held up by the flagger.

Finally, you've had enough and decide to pass a few cars. You bump down onto the old paving in the opposite lane and accelerate. When oncoming traffic appears, you choose a space in front of a slow-mover, brake hard, turn on your right turn signal, and ease the bike back into line on the new paving.

But suddenly, just as your front tire reaches the edge of the new paving, the bike starts falling over, and you can't seem to maintain balance. You lose the struggle and the bike slams onto its side. Fortunately you weren't moving very fast so you just tumble off without getting hurt. But you feel ridiculous dropping your bike in front of the other drivers, and you know without looking that there will be expensive damage.

You should know that raised pavement edges are a special hazard to two-wheelers, and are very common in construction zones. Remember that two-wheelers balance by countersteering the front wheel. If you allow your front tire to ease up next to a raised pavement edge, the tire becomes trapped by the edge and you lose control of balance. It is preferable to simply avoid crossing a raised edge. When you must, it's essential to attack the edge at a minimum angle of 45 degrees, not try to ease over it at a narrow angle. In this situation, you would be wise to stay in line and avoid crossing the edge. If you decide to pass, you should swerve away from the edge of the new pavement and then point the bike back toward the edge at an angle to bounce the front tire up and over.

Falling For You

Making Tight U-Turns Can Be Tricky

You're looking for a place to park at the breakfast meeting. The crowd of riders on the sidewalk turns to look as you glide by. Trouble is, the parking spaces are all taken and the lane comes to an end. You'll have to make a tight U-turn where there isn't much room and you know everyone is watching.

You don't want to embarrass yourself by paddle-walking the bike around like a novice, so you swing as wide as you can, slip the clutch, and try to make a tight circle. However, as the bike swings around, it feels awfully top heavy and won't turn tightly enough. You panic, squeeze the clutch, and stick your leg out, but you can't hold it up. The bike crashes over on its side, and you roll off. Bystanders rush over to help you pick it up. There are only a few scratches in your new paint, and one bruised elbow, but your self-esteem is mortally wounded.

A motorcycle can make a tighter turn when leaned over farther, but to prevent a fall in a tight U-turn, you've got to keep the engine pulling the bike around to keep centrifugal force balanced against gravity. Squeezing the clutch while turning is what causes a bike to topple.

The correct way to make a tight U-turn is to shift your weight onto the outside footpeg to allow you to lean the bike over farther, turn your head to look where you want to go, and ease on just enough throttle to keep the engine pulling all the way around. Avoid squeezing the clutch. The best way to avoid future embarrassments is to practice tight U-turns on your own, preferably out of sight of your friends.

Farm-Road Foul-Ups

It's Tempting to Think of a Backroad As Your Personal Racetrack

You're out on one of those twisty little backcountry roads. The weather's sunny and warm, there's hardly any traffic, the pavement is smooth and clean, and there are a lot of corners. It doesn't get any better than this. You concentrate on delayed-apex lines to maximize your view, and brake at the end of each straight so that you can roll on the throttle as you lean sharply into each curve. You knew you would be getting a little more aggressive on this road, so you're wearing your full leathers as if this were your personal track.

But as you lean over hard into a tight right-hander that carves behind a barn, you realize a tractor is pulling a hay wagon across the road. Instantly you straighten the bike and squeeze as hard as you dare on the front brake. The bike stands on its nose with the front tire shuddering and the rear tire barely touching the pavement. Closing too rapidly on the hay wagon, you squeeze harder, and the front tire suddenly washes out, dumping the bike on its side. Miraculously, you and the bike slide completely under the wagon in a shower of broken plastic. Your leathers save you from any serious road rash, but the bike is a mess.

In the country where traffic is light, farmers and local residents are more complacent about the road. You must constantly remind yourself that a public road isn't your personal racetrack. When in farm country, you should predict that there might be activity near a barn and keep speed down until you can see what is happening. It isn't a farmer's fault if you are riding too fast for a situation. The more aggressively you ride, the more important it is to quickly adjust your speed so that whatever happens you can always stop within your sight distance.

It's Never Too Soon to Work On Your Off-Pavement Skills

You're on your way to a friend's house in the suburbs, and the wide, new street provides a clear view. But as you turn off onto the side street where your friend lives, you realize there are a lot of traffic cones and orange warning signs. Apparently, the side street is being prepared for paving. Your tires bounce off the fresh asphalt onto bumpy dirt, and then into loose gravel. The bike's front wheel starts to plow, first one way and then the other. You instinctively slip the clutch and reach out with your feet to help prevent a spill. When the bike suddenly carves sideways across the loose berm in the center of the lane, you attempt to keep it balanced by countersteering, while you furiously dab with your boots to prevent a spill. But you lose the struggle: the bike slowly topples over. You tumble off, unhurt, but the machine is now scratched, and your ego is severely wounded.

When negotiating slick or loose surfaces, it's helpful to shift more of your body weight to the footpegs—both to place your weight lower on the bike and to allow you to keep the bike more vertical. Attempting to ride the loose gravel with your feet down will contribute to a spill. Choose a track that appears firmest, keep the engine pulling, and have confidence that the bike will plow through. If loose gravel makes you nervous, perhaps you should spend a day on a gravel road to improve your skill and confidence.

Groovy Surprises

A Pavement Groove Can Instantly Wrest Balance Out of Your Control

You're out for a spin on a sunny afternoon. You head for your favorite scenic backroad, eager to get away from traffic and have a spirited ride through the countryside. You know that riding in the city is dangerous for motorcyclists, so you watch the street far ahead to spot potential left-turners, and scrutinize driveways and alleyways for hidden cars about to pull out. It's a relief to finally get faraway and be able to concentrate on the curves.

You discover, however, that the pavement has taken a beating over the winter, and you have to constantly dodge grooves and potholes. You're also surprised to find so many other vehicles on the road. A lot of other sightseers apparently had the same idea as you. There isn't a lot of distance between curves for passing, but by closing up your following distance at the exits of corners, you can pass the gawkers quickly if there's no oncoming traffic. At the moment, you're anxious to get around the slow-moving minivan ahead, so you move up close, shift down to prepare for a quick pass, and focus on the oncoming lane as it comes into view.

Suddenly, your front wheel swerves to the right, and you instinctively wrestle the handlebars toward the left. Before you can recover balance, the bike smashes onto its left side, and you slam into the pavement. You can't believe that two seconds ago you were in control of the bike, and now you're sliding down the asphalt. Apparently, your front tire locked onto the edge of a pavement groove, and you lost control of balance.

It is smart to watch for traffic and avoid passing until you can see there is no oncoming traffic, but whether in city traffic or on the backroads, you must always maintain your awareness of surface hazards. If you observe that a road is in need of repair, you should keep some distance between you and the car in front of you—even if it's a slow mover—to maintain your view of the road surface.

Hidden Turners

Having the Right-of-Way Doesn't Mean You Won't Get Hit

You're riding an arterial street, but traffic is light and you're aware that intersections, alleys, and driveways are locations where accidents frequently occur, so you watch traffic ahead. When you spot vehicles on side streets that might pull out, you cover the brakes and prepare to make a quick stop if needed. You watch especially for oncoming cars that might turn left across your path because you know that left-turners are a major hazard for motorcyclists.

As you approach an intersection, you are watching for such left-turners. There's a large truck to your left waiting to turn left, but as you begin to pass the truck you can see that there are no cars in the opposing lane that could turn left, so you accelerate back to speed to get through the intersection quickly.

Just as you pass the truck, a car suddenly shoots out from the left in front of the truck and directly into your path. You roll off the throttle and swerve hard to avoid a collision. Fortunately, you miss the car, but the rear end slides out and the bike crashes on its side, skidding into the curb in a trail of sparks and broken plastic. The driver speeds away, leaving you to pick yourself up and survey the damage.

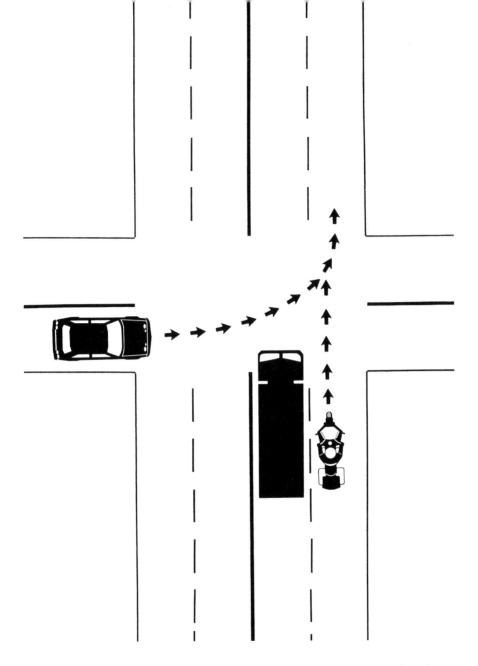

It is wise to understand that intersections are dangerous locations, and it is smart to look for left-turners. But you must predict that a left-turner could be hidden behind a large object such as a truck. Accelerating into an intersection increases forward energy, which increases your stopping distance.

You should always be prepared to stop within your sight distance, which in this case was severely limited by the truck. Even though you may have the legal right-of-way, you should slow down before proceeding until you can see around the object.

High Siding

In a Panic Stop, Overcooking Then Popping the Rear Brake Can Send You Flying

You've taken the bike down to the hardware store for a deep socket, and it's only five miles home on the superslab. Saturday morning traffic is heavy but moving along at a good pace, and you're thinking about getting that oil pressure sender replaced now that you've got the right tool. You notice a compact car towing a trailer with a heavy hard tractor. The trailer and its load appear too large for the small car, and you watch with alarm as the rig sways ahead of you.

Suddenly, just where the freeway curves, the car snaps left, the trailer jackknifes, and both overturn, spitting out the yard tractor. An instant later, drivers around you brake and scatter, their tires smoking. You quickly reach for the front brake and squeeze progressively with all four fingers to allow the weight to transfer forward before applying maximum front brake. Simultaneously, you step down hard on the rear brake pedal, but in the panic you push down too hard, and the rear end slides sideways in the curve. Your survival reaction takes over, and your right foot lets up on the pedal. In a split second, the rear tire grabs the pavement again, snapping the rear end back toward the center so violently that the bike flips. You're catapulted off the bike, which tumbles down the pavement behind you. Miraculously, you slide to a stop without getting run over, and your smart decision to wear your leathers even on a short trip pays off.

Deciding to do a quick stop was smart, too, and your technique to brake progressively helped prevent a front-wheel slideout. Overbraking on the rear should not have prevented you from stopping effectively, even with the rear end sliding sideways. It was your survival reaction to let up on the rear brake that caused the violent high side flip.

While freeways are statistically less hazardous than arterial streets, freeway accidents can occur with little warning, and typically involve chain reactions. If you observe a swaying trailer ahead, you should take immediate action to separate yourself from the problem, not simply watch and wait for the problem to turn into a disaster.

Last Month's Low Tire Pressure Can Turn into Today's Blowout

You and your riding companion are three days into a trip and almost a thousand miles from home now. Your touring machine is loaded to the limits with clothing and camping gear plus some tools and spares. You're amazed at how well the loaded bike handles at speed, now that you've gotten used to the extra weight, and you're very pleased that the bike seldom needs any maintenance.

But over the past couple of days you've noticed a wiggly feel from the rear tire, and you finally decide to pull off at the next rest area to check it. Even though the tire looks a little soft, you don't see any holes or nails. The tread blocks have some strange worn edges, but there's still plenty of rubber and no exposed cords. You suspect the strange feel is just from the extra load, yet decide to have the tire checked anyway if you happen to find a dealer along the way.

Five minutes after leaving the rest area, there's a sickening *bang!* and the rear end starts to wiggle from side to side. Your rear tire has blown, so you ease off the gas, and head for the shoulder. But as your speed drops below 40 mph, the rear end starts to jerk more violently, and you're barely able to bring everything to a stop without dropping the machine. Now you're miles from the rest area where you could've called for help.

When you first notice a wiggling sensation in a tire, pull off the road and try to diagnose a problem. But the damage could have started months before if you allowed your tires to lose air pressure yet continued to ride on them. Underinflated tires can flex enough to heat the cords to destructive temperatures. With an extra load at freeway speeds, it is only a matter of time before a damaged tire comes apart. It's essential to check your tire's pressure with an accurate gauge before each day's ride, especially on long trips. Remember that increased loads require slightly higher tire pressure.

Killer Corner

Every Serpentine Road Has One Special Corner to Challenge Your Skills

Heading home from a weekend trip and taking advantage of sunny weather, you want to add a few enjoyable miles to your adventure by exploring an S-shaped road that parallels the freeway. You're not familiar with this road, but the pavement is smooth and dry, and it curves through the trees with a nice rhythm that encourages you to ride briskly. At the faster pace and reduced sight distance, you know the risks increase, so you scrutinize the road for wild deer or surface hazards, and practice good cornering techniques.

But after a half hour of fun, you're halfway around a blind right turn when you realize it turns even tighter than you had expected. Unlike the hundred other predictable corners you've just ridden, this right-hander tightens up into a decreasing radius and points back up a steep switchback. You try to lean the bike more, but with the bike arcing rapidly toward the opposite shoulder, you panic, roll off the throttle, and slam on the brakes. Both tires slide out, the bike crashes on its side, and you slide off into the ditch in a shower of gravel. You aren't seriously injured, but your bike will require expensive repairs.

Next time you want to do some exploring, keep in mind that most backroads have at least one killer corner, perhaps with an unexpected sharp curve just on the other side of a hill, or an off-camber slant or a decreasing radius. It is wise to look for wild animals and surface hazards, but on an unfamiliar road, it's important to quickly adjust your speed to your sight distance. Approaching a blind turn, you should immediately slow down until you can see the rest of the curve.

If you realize you're going too fast and heading too wide for a turn, the best tactic is to maintain a steady throttle to maximize traction and ground clearance, focus on where you want the bike to go, and push harder on the low grip to lean over to the maximum limits of your machine. On dry pavement, most bikes are capable of turning tighter than their riders realize.

Lane Crashing

Before You Change Lanes, Take a Good Look Around

You're cruising down the freeway in Sunday afternoon traffic, heading for home. With an interchange coming up where you know there will be traffic exiting and merging on the right, you stay in the left lane. But there's a pickup truck ahead of you, cruising in the passing lane. You flash your high beam as a signal that you want to pass, but the driver doesn't seem to notice, so you decide to pass the pickup on the right. You quickly check your mirrors, and flick on the right turn signal as you swing over. Suddenly you realize a car in the right lane is also dodging into the same space. Barely able to swerve, you brake to avoid a collision. It's a close call, and your blood boils at the inconsiderate actions of your fellow motorists.

Yes, it's inconsiderate to cruise in the passing lane or to change lanes without signaling. But remember, the purpose of turn signals is to let other drivers know what you're going to do, not what you're already doing. If you start signaling when you first decide to change lanes, perhaps other drivers will realize your intentions.

It's also up to you to keep from getting run over. When changing lanes, you should always look for traffic in adjacent lanes, and position yourself so that you aren't parallel to other vehicles. Watch especially for cars on the other side of a lane you intend to move into. For example, if you observe a car moving up in the right lane you should predict the driver will be changing lanes, too, even if he or she doesn't signal.

Last Looks

That Last Look over Your Shoulder Before You Pass Can Be a Lifesaver

You have been using your three-wheeler to commute into the big city during the colder months. You know every mile of the suburban highway. The big problem with this state highway is that it's the only major road, and there are few places to pass. This morning, you are caught behind a slow-moving driver who creeps through corners and then speeds up in the straights, making it difficult to pass. But you know there is a long straight coming up just around the next corner. You plan to accelerate up behind the creeper, and if the other lane is clear you'll pull out to pass before the other driver can accelerate.

So you round the corner and see there's no opposing traffic. You signal, continue to accelerate, and pull over into the other lane. Immediately you hear the sound of screeching tires and the blare of a horn, and realize a driver behind you was attempting to pass both you and the creeper on a blind curve. Fortunately, the other driver realizes you were pulling over to pass, and was able to brake quickly enough to avoid a collision.

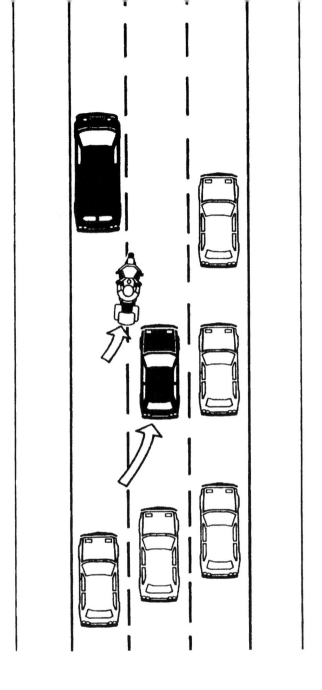

Whenever you decide to pass, take one last look behind you before pulling out. Motorcycles as well as automobiles have blind spots in the mirrors, and turning your head to do a final "shoulder check" can be a lifesaver.

Lethal Lefties

A Big Part of Surviving City Traffic Is Learning to Avoid Left-Turners

You prefer riding your bike on errands, rather than driving the car. You don't usually wear your full riding gear for short trips, but you do wear your helmet and gloves. Today you're on your way to the store to pick up some screws for a home project. Traffic isn't especially heavy this Saturday afternoon, but you discover that the four-lane arterial is being repaved, and your attention is focused on the hazard created by the raised edge of the new paving. You know that even a small edge can cause a spill, so you hold your lane position and a steady 35 mph as you approach an intersection.

Just as you reach the intersection, a car in the opposing left turn lane suddenly accelerates and shoots across your path. You can't believe the driver turned in front of you at the last second! You roll off the throttle, quickly reach for the front brake lever, and squeeze progressively harder as the weight transfers onto the front tire. But before you can get the bike stopped, the bike slams into the car's front fender, the forks folding back under the engine. You're thrown over the hood and onto the pavement. At the hospital, you learn that your left leg is fractured, that you have severe abrasions to your right arm, and that your full-coverage helmet took the brunt of what could have been a fractured jaw. You'll survive, but it's going to be a long time before you ride again.

Even though it's wise to be aware of an edge trap created by new paving, you should not allow the paving hazard to distract you from cars that may be in the opposing left turn lane. They are your greatest hazard. Approaching this type of intersection, you should apply some front brake in anticipation of a quick stop. Just reaching for the brake lever will delay your stop by 50 feet.

Bear in mind that left-turning cars account for about one-fourth of all motorcycle accidents and fatalities in the city, and that the majority of motorcycle accidents occur close to home on short trips. Wear protective riding gear—even on short journeys—to reduce your injuries in case of a crash.

Macadam Muddles

The Key to Identifying Surface Hazards Is Observing Changes in Color or Texture

You've been out for a Sunday ride with some buddies, cruising the backroads on your sportbikes. It was a great day except for a thunderstorm that blew through an hour ago. Now the ride is over, you said, "See you around," at the last coffee stop, and you're heading home. There's still enough daylight to wash the bike and lube the chain before putting it away.

Two blocks from home, you're braking to make a left turn when the bike suddenly starts to fishtail. The rear end slides out to the right, and then whips left and back again, and while you're still fighting for balance, the bike slams onto its side. You aren't hurt, but your fairing is scuffed and the left-side turn signals are dangling. It's a struggle to pick up your bike, and you realize the surface is coated in slippery clay. As you look around, you see a trail of clay tracked out onto the pavement from a nearby construction site. The thundershower earlier had turned it slippery, especially over the plastic lane markings.

Just because your group ride is over doesn't mean your ride is finished. You need to keep your head in your ride in progress until you get home, rather than allowing yourself to get sidetracked by future issues, such as maintenance. You need to always scrutinize the pavement ahead so you can observe a different color and surface texture, and notice such things as slippery clay tracked over the street's shiny plastic letters and arrow.

Once you are aware of a hazard, you can maintain traction by positioning your tires to the left or right of the white plastic surface markings, braking earlier and more gently, and squeezing the clutch to better control rear-wheel braking.

Merging Maniacs

Your Mission Today Is to Get Out of Their Way

You're in the middle of a two-week trip, navigating through a confusing interchange where two interstate highways cross each other. Rounding a corner between two concrete retaining walls, you realize another lane is merging with yours from your left. The signs and pavement markings indicate that your lane has the right-of-way, while traffic in the merging lanes must yield. So, even though you see a car abreast of you in the merging lane, you assume its driver intends to yield.

But where the lanes come together, the other driver doesn't slow down to move out of your way. Instead, the driver steps on the gas and tries to pull over in front of you. You beep your horn and instinctively swerve right to avoid a collision, but it's just too close. The rear fender of the car taps the bike, knocking it off the pavement onto the ditch. After the crash you're still conscious, but from the pain, you know your trip is over. The driver stops, calls for emergency help, admits fault, and apologizes, but you are the one who is injured, miles from home.

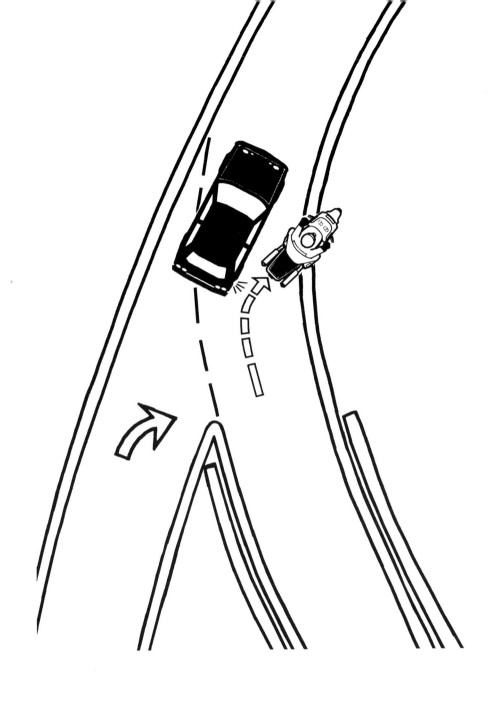

You may not be legally at fault in such an accident, but it is little consolation if the other driver admits fault when it's you who's in pain. And some drivers don't even stop after an accident. When you observe another car on a collision course with you, never assume that the driver sees you or intends to yield the right-of-way. In this situation, you should accelerate or brake to put yourself in a better position to avoid a collision.

Neighborhood Dogs

Outsmarting Free-Roaming Canines

You're cruising along a shady side street in the 'burbs. It's a warm afternoon, traffic is light, and you're in no hurry. Suddenly you're aware of an animal running toward you from a side yard. The dog's ears are back, its teeth are bared, and its tail is down. You prepare to kick at the dog if it tries to bite you. But the dog sprints out fast enough to intercept your path just beyond a parked car. He leaps into the street, running alongside your front wheel, snarling, and snapping just out of reach of your kicks. To your surprise, he darts under your front wheel, the tire flips up, and you lose balance and fall. The dog limps off, leaving you to deal with a damaged bike and scuffed riding gear.

Loose dogs are a huge problem in many neighborhoods. You should know how they show aggression. Be aware that a large dog's teeth are sharp enough to penetrate fabric riding gear, and that even a small dog can upset a motorcycle by getting under the front wheel.

Rather than trying to defend yourself by kicking, you should outsmart the dog. Most motorcycles can accelerate faster than a canine. When you see a loose dog running toward you, slow down to give the dog the idea that there is no hurry getting to the point of interception. Then shift down, and as it gets closer, accelerate quickly out of reach.

However, if you encounter the same dog time after time, it will quickly learn to adapt to your trick. You could consider a different route, but it would be better for you to talk with the dog's owner or initiate a complaint to the animal control office.

Off-Ramp Get-Offs

78

Quick Stops in a Curve Require Both Knowledge and Skill

You're using the bike more and more to commute to work in order to use the carpool lanes. There's an increased hazard of riding during the rush hours, but you always look as far ahead as possible, cover the front brake, and wear full protective gear. This morning, traffic is heavy but moving along nicely. With your exit coming up, you signal and change lanes toward the right-hand off-ramp. There's a gaggle of aggressive commuters taking this exit and other cars attempting to enter the freeway at the same point, but you are able to merge into line and make your turnoff.

The trees next to the off-ramp limit your view, so you don't see the brake lights suddenly come on until you're halfway around the exit ramp. Closing rapidly on the car ahead, you roll off the throttle and squeeze hard on the front brake to make a quick stop. But with the bike leaned over into the curve, the front wheel loses its grip, the bike crashes on its low side, and slams out into the guard rail. Fortunately, the drivers behind you see what's happening and avoid running over you.

Since risks are higher in heavy traffic, it is smart to wear protective gear for commuting. And it's also a good habit to cover the front brake lever in potentially hazardous situations where you may need to make a sudden stop. But you shouldn't allow yourself to get so close to the car ahead of you, especially where the view is limited. Braking while leaned over requires considerable skill, even if your bike has ABS. Rather than attempt to brake hard while still leaned over, you can quickly swerve the bike upright and then attempt a maximum-effort straight-line stop.

Oily On

Spilled Diesel Oil Is a Major Surface Hazard for Motorcyclists

You're headed for the Sunday breakfast meeting, running a little late, but a quick transit on the freeway will get you there in time. The sun is just starting to warm the air and dry the morning dew off the pavement. Rounding the freeway on-ramp, you lean the bike into the curve, roll on the gas to accelerate to freeway speed, and turn your head to watch for traffic. You catch a brief whiff of petroleum in the air, but your attention is focused on merging onto the freeway. You don't see any traffic, so you continue to accelerate.

Suddenly the big tourer slips sideways. The tires aren't howling, just sliding, as if some invisible hand had shoved the bike sideways. Then, just as suddenly, the tires regain traction, and you fight for control as the bike snaps violently from side to side. Rolling off the gas, you drift over to the shoulder and stop, your hands shaking from the near-disaster. You expect to find a flat tire. But apparently there's nothing wrong with the bike. Then you smell petroleum again, and realize there's a slippery liquid on your tires. Looking back at the on-ramp, you now see the oily sheen of spilled diesel oil seeping downhill from the center of the lane. You had done everything right except scrutinize the road surface.

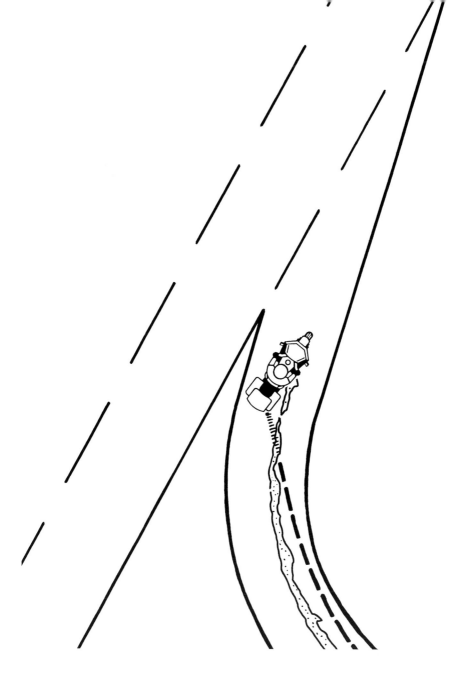

While it is important to check for traffic before merging, it's also important to maintain your awareness of road surface hazards. On-ramps are notorious for fuel spills because fluids tend to spill from full tanks as vehicles round the tight turns. An odor of petroleum is an important clue you shouldn't ignore. You can usually see a slightly darker color on the road or a rainbow-colored sheen of spilled oil. Since liquids tend to seep downhill, one precaution is to favor the uphill wheel track and avoid the center of the lane whenever you suspect a spill.

One-Way Weasels

Stay Away from Sleepy Drivers on One-Way Streets

You've been planning a big trip for weeks. You loaded the bike last night, and this morning you're working your way out of town through commuter traffic. You'll be glad to get out on the open road where you can finally settle into the ride and burn some miles. You move to the left lane of the narrow one-way street to pass a slower-moving car.

But just as you're about to pass the car, the driver starts to turn left, right across your path. You can't believe the driver is turning left from the right lane! You roll off the gas, squeeze the clutch, and squeeze progressively harder on the front brake as the touring load transfers onto the front tire. You manage to slow just enough to miss the car's rear bumper, and the driver continues the turn, proceeding on down the street as if nothing had happened.

You're furious, until you realize that you were in the driver's left rear blind spot when approaching an intersection. The sleepy driver may not have realized he was on a one-way street, didn't see anyone in the other lane, and wasn't looking for a motorcycle to his left.

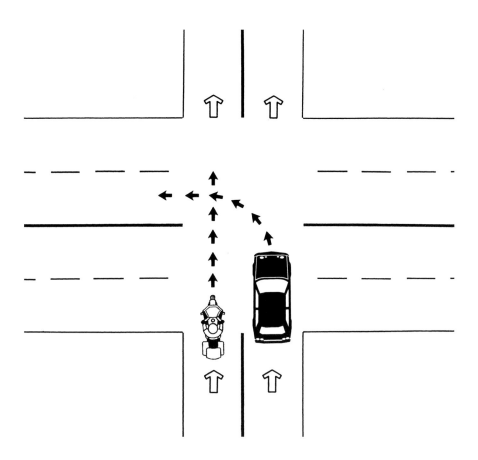

Practicing your quick-stop braking will pay off in situations like this by preparing you to avoid a collision through maximum-effort braking. It is smart to move out from behind a slower-moving vehicle, but you should observe an approaching intersection and stay out of another driver's blind spot. It's seldom wise to ride parallel to another vehicle in traffic, even if you think the other driver can see you.

It's a better idea to either stay behind a slower car until you are through the intersection, or to pass the car earlier and pull ahead of it between intersections. Furthermore, it's not a good tactic to accelerate while approaching an intersection because increasing speed greatly increases stopping distance.

Parking Lot Darters

Don't Expect Drivers to Follow Street-Traffic Rules in Private Parking Lots

You've done some shopping at the mall, and now you're leaving the parking lot. Riding down the lane between the parked cars, you scan your mirrors to check for tailgaters, watch carefully for pedestrians who might jump out of their cars, and look for backup lights that warn of someone about to reverse. You understand that parking-lot intersections are just as dangerous as street corners, so you scrutinize the cross-traffic ahead, and plan to make a full stop when you get there.

But before you reach the end of the row, a car suddenly darts out from behind a van. With barely two seconds before impact, there isn't time to grab for the brakes. You push on the grip to try to swerve out of the way of the darter, but you can't stop in time to avoid a glancing blow off the bumper of a parked car. The darter roars off. Luckily, you suffer from only abrasions and bruises, but you're left with responsibility for the collision.

Since private parking lots are not part of the public streets, there's no police enforcement for ignoring lane markings or signs. Therefore, many drivers don't obey street-traffic rules in large parking lots. Not only is it wise to watch carefully for pedestrians and backing cars, but you should also predict the hazard of vehicles darting through empty parking spaces. When riding through parking lots, always scan the adjacent lanes and be prepared to make a quick stop by keeping your speed down. Also, shorten your stopping distance by covering the front brake lever.

Passing Panic

Passing a Delivery Truck on a Side Road Can Be the End of Your Ride

It's an outstanding day for your favorite scenic highway. Saturday morning traffic has been light, the weather is sunny and warm, and the bike is running great. You've been enjoying the old highway at a comfortable pace. The only negative in an otherwise great ride is a delivery truck that you've been following for the last few miles. The driver speeds up and then brakes for no apparent reason. You'd like to pass, but the truck blocks your view of the road ahead.

Finally, you hang over the centerline just enough to see a straightaway with no one in the opposing lane. You signal, shift down, do a quick shoulder check, and accelerate as you pull over to pass. But just as you're almost even with the back of the truck, it suddenly slows and starts moving across the centerline toward you. You're shocked to realize the truck is turning left into a driveway. You brake to the limits of traction without skidding your tires, and manage to bring the bike to a stop inches from the truck as it continues into the driveway.

Erratic driving by a truck driver should be a clue that the driver is looking for an address and not focusing on a motorcycle behind him or her. If the truck slows down, it's a clue that the driver might be about to make a turn. While it seems that the straightaway would be a good place to pass in this story and illustration, you should observe the driveway on the left and predict the possibility of the truck making a left turn. While quick-stop skills would enable you to avoid a collision, better predicting skills could help you avoid the hazard in the first place.

Pendulous Passes

If You're Going to Pass, Get Prepared to Move Along

Your Sunday ride has been enjoyable except for slow-moving tourists on the road. The state highway winds through wooded hills with glimpses of farms. But a slow-moving car ahead is holding up several cars, and there are few passing zones where drivers can get around the slow mover. You know there's a straight stretch coming up, and you decide to pass the whole group at once if the opposing lane is clear. Thankfully, there are no approaching vehicles, so you signal, check your mirrors, pull out to pass, and roll on the throttle.

But when you roll it on, you realize the bike is still in top gear, and it accelerates very sluggishly for several seconds until the engine gets up into the power band. You're not quite past the middle of the pack as you see the double yellow line starting just ahead, with a car coming around the corner. You brake hard to swerve back in line, but the other drivers haven't left you any space. You're barely able to squeeze over onto the yellow lines as the opposing car whizzes by.

When passing, it's important to accelerate as quickly as possible to reduce the time you're in the wrong lane. But if you realize the bike isn't accelerating as quickly as you'd like it to, you should immediately shift down or change your plan. You can decide to pass only one car or abort the pass, pull back in line, and wait for another passing zone when you can be better prepared. A slow acceleration at the beginning of a pass can result in a panic situation at the end.

Peppery Passes

Before You Change Lanes, It's a Good Idea to Know What's Around You

You've finally found some time to take that cross-country trip to the big motorcycle rally, and now you're just trying to get out of the big city. Morning rush-hour traffic is heavy, and you're being held up in the left lane by some tourists in a slow-moving van. You flash your high beam as a signal that you want to pass, but the driver is oblivious. After a few seconds, you decide to pass on the right. Quickly you signal, check your right mirror, and start to move over.

Suddenly a horn is blaring right behind you, and you realize you're about to collide with a car. You manage to swerve back over the line just in time to avoid being sideswiped as the driver accelerates by, glaring at you. You're angered at the other driver's aggression and embarrassed at not noticing the car was so close.

The other driver had come up from behind, elbowing his way through traffic. He had momentarily pulled into the left lane behind you, but decided to make a quick pass to the right at the same time you did. The driver didn't see your late signal until he was already changing lanes and didn't care.

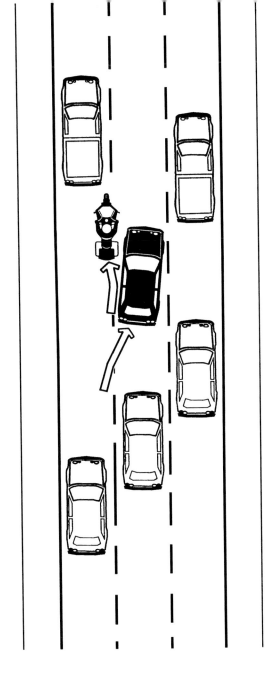

You should expect aggressive drivers on today's highways to move at much higher speeds than average, pass on the right, and make multiple lane changes without signaling. To avoid being a victim of such road sharks, maintain your awareness of the dynamic patterns of vehicles all around you, including those behind you. To help other motorists understand your intentions, you should signal at least three seconds prior to a lane change. And before you change lanes, it's smart to actually turn your head and scan the lane in which you intend to go.

Poor Predicting

If You Guess Wrong, You Can Morph a Near Miss into a Collision

You're on your way home after a quick Saturday afternoon trip to the store. Traffic on the urban arterial is heavy with a lot of drivers making left turns into businesses. You're aware that left-turning cars are a big hazard for motorcyclists, so you scrutinize oncoming vehicles for clues that they may be turning across your path, and you cover the front brake lever in case you need to make a panic stop.

You're not surprised when you see an oncoming car starting to turn left. The driver doesn't signal, but you see the hood dip slightly, and the front wheel start to turn in your direction. You know what's happening, so you're in no danger, but you are indignant that the driver doesn't seem to care. You predict that there will be just enough space for you to cut close behind the offending driver as he continues into the parking lot. You intend to ride straight ahead and then beep your horn as a wake-up call.

But halfway across your path, the driver suddenly sees you and slams on the brakes. Pushing hard on the left grip, you're barely able to swerve around the car, missing the rear bumper by inches. Now you're really angry at the driver's stupidity.

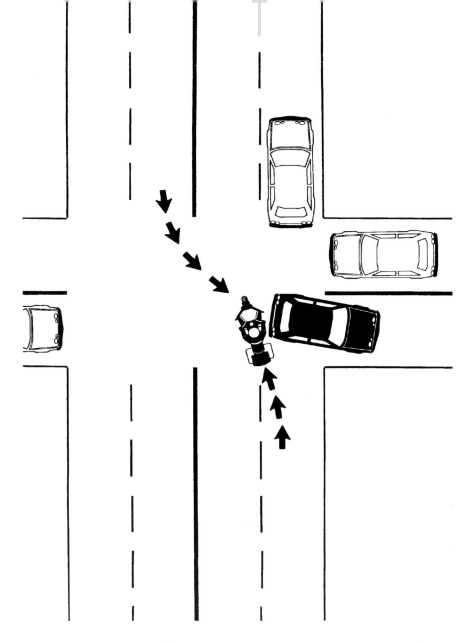

Approximately one-fourth of all motorcycle accidents are collisions with left-turners, so being aware of possible left-turners is wise. But you can't assume that a driver turning across your path sees you. And you can't predict that the driver will continue into the parking lot across your path if he or she suddenly sees you at the last minute. You need to be ready to make a quick stop in case that driver panics and stops in your path. You should also be aware of other vehicles that could pull out into your path, such as a driver waiting to pull out from your right. In this situation, you can improve your odds by ignoring the unintentional transgression and using your knowledge and skill to create more separation.

Pushy Passengers

Change Your Riding Techniques When Carrying a Passenger

Most of the time you ride by yourself, but one of your coworkers has expressed an interest in motorcycling, and you've agreed to take her for a Sunday afternoon ride. You provide the riding gear, including a helmet that fits properly, a riding jacket, and leather gloves. You also explain what to expect on the ride, and take it easy for the first hour to allow her to get comfortable gradually. Now that your passenger has relaxed and is enjoying the ride, you gradually increase speed, carving through the corners on this shady backroad.

Up ahead you observe a deer grazing alongside the road. As you get closer, the deer raises its head and suddenly leaps out of the ditch into your path. You reach for the front brake and attempt a quick stop. But as you brake harder, your passenger slams into your back, and you realize you can't brake as hard as you need to without being pushed up onto the tank. You manage to miss the deer by inches, but the experience still leaves you shaking and your passenger frightened.

Although it is smart to provide proper riding gear and give a new passenger time to adapt to a motorcycle, you also should realize that extra weight effects performance, including your ability to make a quick stop. If you're carrying a new passenger, it's a good idea to ride more conservatively for the entire trip. And if you do spot a deer on your ride, you should immediately apply the brakes instead of waiting until the situation turns into a panic. Remember that with a passenger you can use more rear brake than when riding solo because there's more weight on the rear tire. But you should still plan for longer stopping distances when carrying a passenger.

Railroad Tracks

You Need to Be Cautious When Crossing Steel Rails

You're riding in the right lane of a four-lane arterial street in an industrial area of the city. When you see the right lane ending ahead, you check in the mirror for an opening in traffic and ease over toward the left lane. Suddenly the bike slides sideways and you struggle to maintain balance, then you realize there's a railroad spur crossing the street right where you attempted to change lanes. You were wise to watch for traffic before merging with the other lane, but you should also have been watching the road surface.

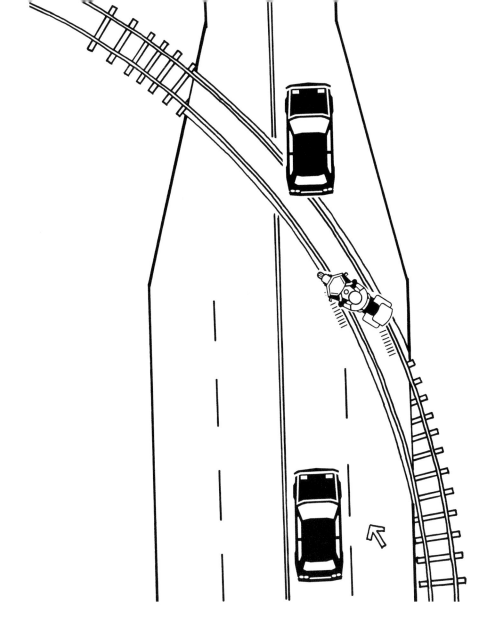

Noncollision spills are a common type of motorcycle accident, and spills are frequently a result of surface hazards. Railroad sidings are common in industrial areas. Shiny steel rails can easily cause the front tire to slide, and it is difficult to control balance when front tire traction is lost. Some track crossings have deep grooves that can actually grab the tires and wrench the handlebars out of your grasp.

When crossing railroad tracks, it's always wise to adjust your path of travel to cross the rails at an angle of 45 degrees or greater with the motorcycle upright and stabilized in a straight line. In this particular situation, you should observe the rails ahead, move over to the left lane, and then adjust your line to cross the rails at more of an angle.

If You Can't See Them, They Probably Can't See You

You're riding in the left lane of a familiar four-lane urban arterial. You know that in city traffic, left-turning autos are a major hazard, so you scrutinize oncoming vehicles and side streets for possible left-turners who might suddenly dart across your path. Ahead of you in the right lane is a large commercial truck, and you're gaining on it. You know that trucks and busses block the view, so you plan to accelerate and quickly pass the truck.

But just as you are pulling ahead of the truck cab, a car suddenly appears from the right in front of the truck and swerves into your lane. You instinctively push left and roll off the gas to avoid a collision. You miss the car, but the rear wheel loses traction, slides right, snaps left, and hits the pavement in a shower of sparks and plastic. As you tumble to a stop, you see the car driver speeding away. Fortunately, the vehicles behind you are able to stop quickly. You realize the car must have accelerated out of a right-hand side street, passed in front of the truck, and swerved into your lane to avoid getting hit by the truck.

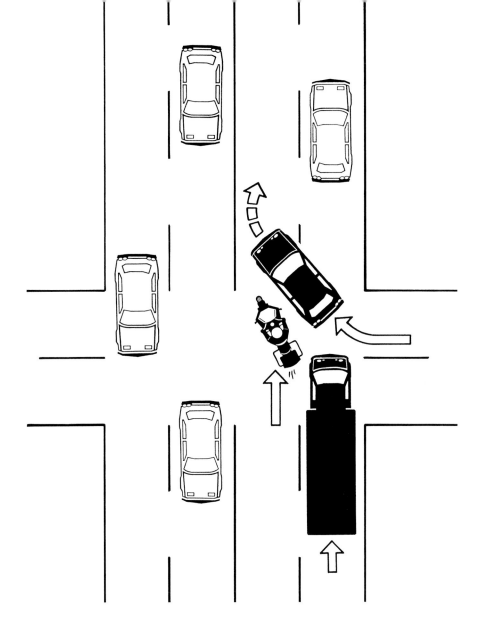

Even though left-turning cars are a significant traffic hazard and even though it's smart to take steps to separate yourself from a view-blocking commercial truck, you should be aware that impatient drivers on side streets may attempt to pull out in front of a truck or bus. When you're passing any large vehicle—whether to the right or left and whether moving or stopped—it's best to prepare for a stop until you can clearly see that no other vehicles are in the process of turning or changing lanes. And remember, swerving without falling requires that you control your "survival" urge to snap off the throttle or jam on the brakes at the same time. Hard braking in a straight line is a better tactic than attempting to swerve.

A Little Rainwater on the Road Turns the Surface into a Slippery Mess

It's Saturday morning, and you can't wait to get the bike out for a ride. The sun is shining, the sky is blue, and the air is calm and warm. It's a perfect day to go exploring the foothills, before tomorrow's storm front blows in from the west.

By noon, you're miles from home and a little surprised that dark clouds are starting to move in sooner than the forecast had predicted. When you see raindrops starting to dampen the restaurant parking lot, you reluctantly decide to cut the ride short and head home before the streets get really wet.

Taking a more direct route along an urban arterial, you can't believe how slippery the road is in such a light rain. When you stop for a red light, you're shocked when both tires begin to slide, and you barely manage to keep the bike upright as it finally stops halfway into the crosswalk. By the time you turn into your driveway, the slick streets have you really paranoid.

City streets are extremely slippery during the first few minutes of a fresh rain, as the accumulated "road gorp" emulsifies with water. It takes about a half hour of steady downpour to completely wash the accumulated oil off the pavement. Increasing your speed also demands more traction at a time when traction is poor. Rather than try to hurry home, the safer tactic is to stop for a leisurely lunch and allow time for the rain to wash the road surface.

There's No Lack of Aggressive Drivers on the Road These Days

You're cruising down the freeway on your way home from the Sunday breakfast meeting. You're in no hurry, but you maintain a slightly higher speed than the traffic's average. You know that accidents can happen quickly on the freeway, so you scan the situation far ahead to spot problems. And you usually avoid the right hand lane, to stay out of merging traffic.

You follow a slow-moving pickup truck in the left lane for a few moments, and then decide to move over to the center lane and pass the truck on the right. You signal, look over your right shoulder to be sure there isn't anyone in your blind spot, change lanes, and start to accelerate.

But suddenly a car in the left lane passes you and swerves into the center lane without signaling. You roll off the throttle and swerve right, barely managing to avoid a collision. The car squeezes between you and the truck and roars away. You see the driver glance at you in his rearview mirror, so you know he saw you. You're incensed that a pushy driver would threaten your life by such a reckless pass.

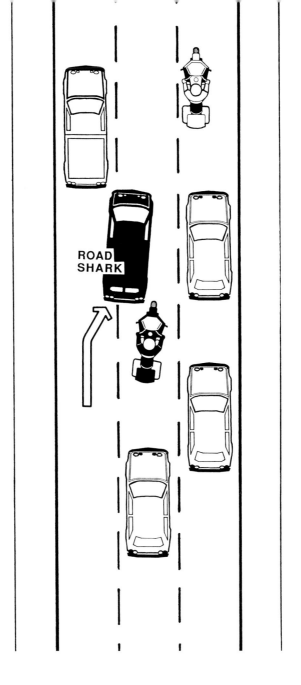

ROAD
SHARK

It's always smart to look far ahead in traffic, but you must maintain your awareness of other vehicles all around you, not just in front. If you monitor the traffic behind you, you can spot road sharks, like the driver in this story, weaving through traffic, frequently changing lanes. If you see a car accelerating toward a slow-moving vehicle in its lane, you can predict that it will suddenly change lanes, so you can stay out of its way.

Rolling Stops

Clever Riders Always Plan On a Complete Stop at Stop Signs

You're approaching a busy intersection from a side street. Your street has a Stop sign. Immediately, you observe a gap in the oncoming traffic where you can make your right turn—if you don't waste any time. You quickly slow almost to a stop, and then immediately make your turn into traffic. But just as you begin to turn, a car changes lanes into your path. You aren't moving fast enough to swerve out of the way, and you aren't prepared to do a quick stop, especially while leaned over. The bike ricochets off the front fender of the car, and the accident is your fault.

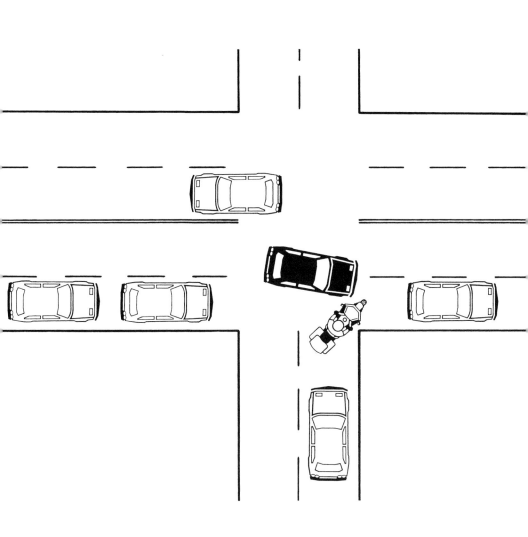

Rushing into intersections isn't wise. If you're not prepared for a stop when you realize your path is blocked, it's difficult to keep the bike under control. Even a brief stop would give you time to evaluate the situation and observe a car moving into your intended lane. Remember that more motorcyclists are injured and killed at intersections than at any other location.

The best way to be prepared for surprises in situations such as this is to come to a complete stop at all Stop signs, with your left foot supporting the motorcycle and your right foot on the brake pedal. Keeping your foot on the rear brake not only keeps the bike from creeping ahead but also illuminates the brake light to signal traffic behind you.

Expect Impatient Drivers to Bull Their Way Through Intersections

You're returning home from the hardware store, riding a narrow two-lane side street. Traffic is busy as other people dash around completing their shopping. You know that the risks of collisions are high on Saturday afternoon, so you maintain a reasonable speed and watch carefully for other vehicles.

At a four-way stop, you observe three other cars also approaching the intersection. Since you arrived at the intersection first, you assume you'll proceed first, yet you quickly check the vehicles ahead of you and to your right to make sure they intend to wait for you. You also look at the driver on your left, and establish eye contact.

But, just as you ease out the clutch to continue through the intersection, the driver on your left suddenly steps on the gas and swerves into a left turn, then slams on the brakes and stops, right in your path. Your front wheel plows into the car's passenger door. It's a slow-speed collision, and you aren't seriously injured, but you can't believe what this driver did.

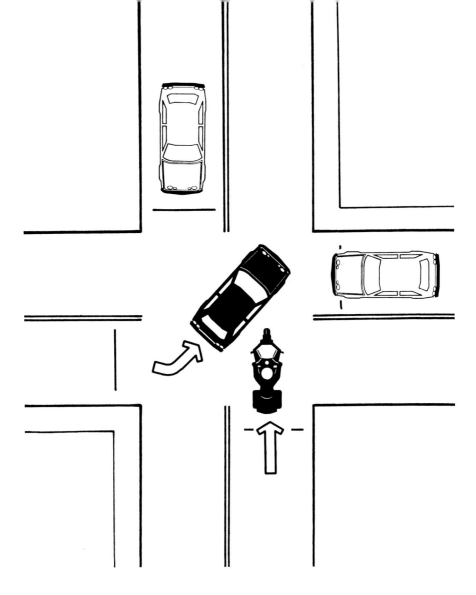

Of course, it is wise to keep your speed down in busy weekend traffic, use caution at a four-way intersection, and to look for potential left-turners. But automobile drivers are often in too much of a hurry to yield the right-of-way to a motorcycle. Establishing eye contact doesn't guarantee that the driver to your left will give you the right-of-way. This driver might not realize that motorcycles follow the same rules as automobiles or might have assumed that swiveling your helmet around was a signal to proceed.

Whenever there is a question about right-of-way, maintain light contact with the front brake even as you start to move to reduce reaction time in the event you need to stop quickly. Even if you arrive at a four-way intersection first, you should be prepared to stop for any of the three other vehicles.

For That First Spring Ride, Remember the Surface Hazards

It's been a long, cold winter in your part of the country, and when the first warm spring day finally arrives, you're eager to go for a ride. The bike is coaxed to life, you get into your gear, and you're off. It feels strange riding a two-wheeler again after a winter of driving the car to work. But it's good being back in the saddle, and your riding skills quickly return. You'd almost forgotten how much fun it is to leave other vehicles behind as you squirt away from signal lights and lean over sharply to power around corners.

You are especially aware of your vulnerability in riding a motorcycle in traffic, and you try to remember such tactics as staying out of other drivers' blind spots, avoiding the grease strip in the center of turn lanes, and being prepared to avoid left-turning vehicles at intersections. Approaching an arterial from a side street, you scrutinize traffic, looking for an opening.

There's just enough room to pull out in front of a pickup truck if you don't dawdle. But as you accelerate onto the arterial, the rear end of the bike suddenly slides sideways. You barely maintain balance by wild countersteering, and the truck driver has to slow down to avoid you. Quite embarrassing.

Coasting over to the side of the street to look for a problem with the bike, you realize there's a layer of sand at the corner, left over from wintertime street sanding. When you attempted to accelerate through the turn, the rear tire lost traction on the sand.

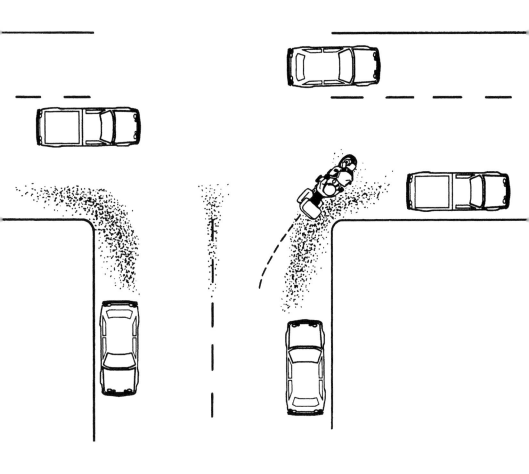

You must never forget how important it is for a motorcyclist to be aware of surface hazards. In climates where sanding streets in winter is common, you can expect loose sand to be present each spring. The sand typically gets pushed toward the outside of lanes by passing traffic. Be especially wary of sand at intersections where it often collects in a berm near the curb.

When driving in springtime, avoid the urge to make a quick pullout, and take extra seconds to scrutinize the street surface. You may be able to avoid the sand by making a wider turn, farther from the curb. If you can't avoid crossing a patch of loose sand on the pavement, keep your motorcycle more vertical, and avoid rapid acceleration, hard braking, or sharp turns while driving through it.

Shark Repellent

Protecting Yourself from Aggressive Drivers

You're riding a familiar two-lane highway that is often clogged with tourists during the summer months. In fact, at this very moment, you're being held up by a carload of gawkers, which you're looking for an opportunity to get around. Because of the curves, there are very few places to pass, but you know there is a straightaway coming up. However, when you scrutinize the passing zone, you see traffic in the other lane and decide against it. You've learned to be patient on this road after seeing a number of close calls when overeager drivers took chances trying to pass slow-moving vehicles. What's more, you don't like the looks of an oncoming tailgating road shark who's driving aggressively, darting over the centerline, apparently looking for a hole to squeeze through.

You realize that the shark might dart over to pass a slow mover after the car ahead of you goes by. You also suspect that such an aggressive driver might not be expecting or looking for a motorcycle. To position yourself farther away from a possible sideswipe you move over to the right side of your lane. Sure enough, as soon as the oncoming car has gone by, the shark immediately swerves over to pass. Had you stayed in the left side of your lane, you very likely would have been hit.

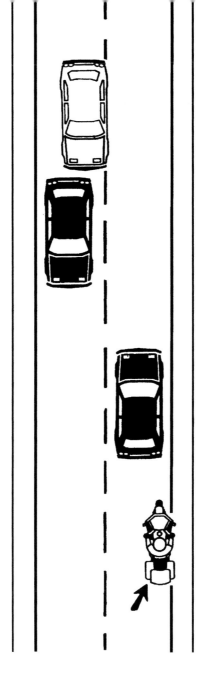

You can avoid potentially fatal accidents by scrutinizing the road ahead, observing aggressive road sharks, and taking evasive action before situations become critical. Moving toward the right side of the lane in a situation like this one may reduce your conspicuity but increases your separation from a potential hazard and may save your life.

Shocking Truths

Sacked Suspension Isn't Just a Matter of Comfort

You're out for a ride in the country on a bike that you've owned for a number of years; in fact, it still has most of its original parts. You understand the importance of good tires, so you buy the best and check tire pressure before every ride. This curving road through farmland is one of your favorites because it's usually free of other vehicles, and you can ride it at an energetic pace, carving through shady river bottoms and snaking back up the bluffs.

Like most secondary backroads, the pavement receives little attention from maintenance crews, so you're careful to skirt potholes and frost heaves where the asphalt paving is crumbling and to watch for wet leaves. But the surface appears good approaching a sweeping turn under the flickering canopy of tall trees, so you roll on more throttle and lean the bike over to a more aggressive angle. Suddenly the wheels begin to hammer into a series of pavement ridges hidden by the shadows, and the bike chatters sideways. You instinctively roll off the gas, but can't avoid drifting wide and plowing into the muddy roadside ditch. You aren't hurt, but the bike's a mess.

Even though it's smart to invest in new tires, you also need to maintain your suspensions. You can't expect the original factory shock absorbers and springs on an old machine to keep up the bike in the middle of its suspension travel over pavement ripples. Considering the advances in suspension design over the years, it might be time to start looking at a more contemporary machine.

Side Street Sideswipe

Quiet Side Streets Can Lull You into a False Sense of Security

You're returning home from a Sunday ride. The weather is balmy, and there are few cars moving on the side streets that lead you home. Now that you're out of the freeway craziness, you can relax and savor the last few minutes of the ride. The bike performed flawlessly, and you can't wait for next weekend. You've got time to wash and polish it before dinner, and maybe you'll even treat it to new tires before the next ride.

Then a curious glint of reflected sun from the other side of the hill awakens you from your reverie. Suddenly there's a car hurtling toward you in the center of the narrow street. You instinctively swerve right to avoid a head-on collision, even while you're reaching for the brake lever. Before you can swerve entirely out of the way, the car fender slams into your left saddlebag, instantly pushing the rear of the bike out from under you. Your bike slides into a parked car, denting the bottom of a door. The wide-eyed teenage driver panics and roars off without stopping. Luckily, you avoid serious injury, but now you'll have to track down the owner of the parked car, report the accident to the police, and go through the headache of getting your bike repaired.

It's easy to allow yourself to be lulled into a false sense of security by the relative quiet of a side street. But you should expect to see other vehicles and recognize a situation as being hazardous if, say, there is a hill limiting your view and parked cars, reducing your escape options. In such a situation you can move over to the right just before the crest of the hill and pause until you can determine that there is no oncoming traffic.

Signaling Slipups

It's Easier Than You Think to Misinterpret Signals

You're on your way home from a ride in the country. You smile as you remember that great section of winding road that you turned around and rode again, just for fun. But now you're almost home, so it's time to start thinking about the projects you need to finish.

The next right turn after the gas station will take you down your street, and four blocks later, you'll be pulling up to your garage and zipping off your riding gear. There's a car parked at the gas station, but there aren't any vehicles entering or leaving your street. You flick on the right turn signal just in case someone else should appear or the police happen to be watching.

But just as you start to lean the bike over toward your street, that car pulls out of the gas station, right into your path. You can see the driver looking at you, but he pulls out in front of you anyway. Luckily, you always use the front brake as part of your cornering sequence, so you instinctively squeeze harder on the lever. The bike stops inches short of a collision and the other driver roars away. You're furious until you realize that you may have caused the problem yourself. Signaling for the right turn could have been misinterpreted to mean that you were turning into the gas station, not down the adjacent street.

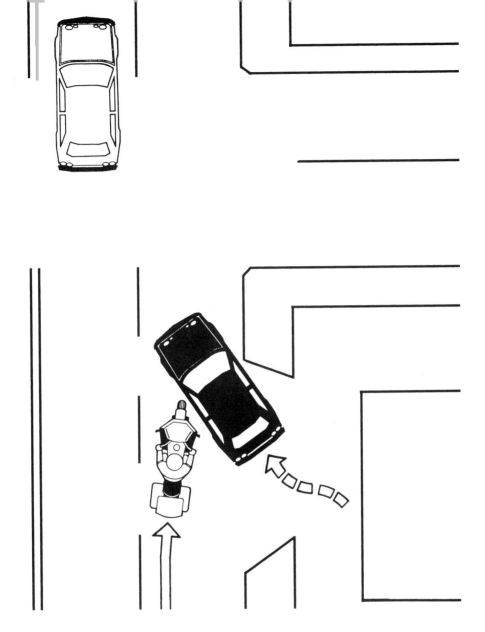

Squeezing on a little front brake when approaching turns is a good tactic. In this situation, it reduced the reaction time just enough to avoid what could have been a nasty crash. And signaling your intentions well in advance is generally a good idea. But allowing your mind to wander while riding is a dangerous habit. You should always be thinking about the possible actions of drivers around you and how they might interpret your signals so you can take evasive action. If a driver is waiting to pull out right before your turn, you should delay signaling until you are closer to your turn or slow and give the other driver a wave to proceed in front of you and then continue around the corner.

Take a Break When It First Starts to Rain

Relieved to be off the freeway, you're almost home when gray skies start to sprinkle for the first time in a month. Crossing the wet bricks of an old section of street, you keep the bike as upright as possible to avoid sliding out. You're also careful to ride to one side of a slippery white arrow on the surface of a one-way street. And you back off to provide more space between your bike and vehicles ahead.

As you approach an intersection, the signal light changes to red more quickly than other drivers had anticipated, and suddenly the car ahead of you is fishtailing to a stop. You apply the rear brake gently and squeeze the front lever progressively, but the front tire skids on the slippery pavement, and the bike slams over on its side. You aren't hurt, and other drivers manage to avoid hitting your fallen machine, but the bike is a mess: Mirrors are broken, mufflers are scraped, and the fairing is cracked. You're infuriated about the rain, the slick street, and other drivers' carelessness.

When it starts to rain close to your destination, the temptation is to hurry. But be aware that when it hasn't rained for at least a month, pavement is most slippery during that first half hour of rain. And even if you are close to home, you should consider stopping for a break to allow a few minutes for the accumulated slippery goo to wash off the road surface.

When approaching a controlled intersection on wet pavement, always allow greater following distance, ride in the left-wheel track rather than the greasy center of the lane, and be more aware of what's happening at the intersection ahead. When you do need to make a quick stop on a slippery surface, you should apply the front and rear brakes equally.

Keeping Your Front Tire Planted on Those Uphill Corners

You and your passenger have managed to break away from work long enough for that big road trip to the West Coast, and you're both riding your bike on a twisty highway through the hills above the ocean. The road dips down into valleys and climbs steeply up the hilly canyons, snaking around hundreds of tight switchbacks. This is exactly the way you had dreamed about the Coast and its canyon roads, and you ride aggressively, enjoying every curve, every minute.

What your dreams didn't include are the slower vehicles blocking your swift progress, such as that old van ahead. It isn't easy to pass because sight distance is always limited. Finally, you reach a sweeping curve where you can see the road is clear, and you roll on the throttle to pass. But passing seems to anger the van driver, who stomps on the gas and tries to outrun you. To avoid a confrontation, you speed up a bit to gain some distance.

Approaching a very tight right-hand uphill switchback, you slow down for the turn, and then roll on the throttle to pull the bike up the steep hill. But as you roll on the gas, the front tire suddenly chirps sideways. You barely manage to maintain balance and avoid a slideout, but the bike drifts over into the opposing lane. Luckily, no one is coming downhill. You manage to recover and stay ahead of the aggressive van driver for the next few miles, but the situation certainly got your attention.

When you have a passenger on your bike, it affects how you handle hills and corners. Remember, a passenger adds more mass that must be pushed uphill, and that lightens the front end, reducing front-tire traction. If you slow down too early and then suddenly roll on the throttle in a tight uphill turn, you'll lighten the front end just when you need traction on the front tire to get the bike turned.

You can enter an uphill turn at a higher speed than at level turns because your increased forward energy helps overcome gravity pulling backward on the machine. Enter a turn close to the outside of your lane, and get the bike turned while inertia is still pushing it uphill and the front tire still has traction. Then, when the motorcycle is pointed uphill, ease on the throttle progressively to help avoid a wheelie.

If You're Sliding Your Tires, You're Not Stopping in the Shortest Distance

You're on your way home from a Sunday afternoon ride. Freeway traffic back into the city is crazy, with drivers accelerating and then suddenly braking as traffic surges faster and slower. In such situations you just roll on and off the throttle and occasionally use a little rear brake. Finally, you reach your exit and get onto familiar city streets. The frequent stoplights are a bother, but at least they're predictable.

Then, as you decelerate for a red light, a pickup truck in the next lane suddenly swerves over in front of you, the driver jamming on the brakes. Instinctively, you step down hard on the rear brake pedal, the rear tire squealing and smoking as it tries to drag the bike to a stop. It's all you can do to keep the bike upright as your front tire slams into the rear bumper of the truck. You aren't hurt, but your front wheel is bent and you're at fault because you rear-ended the truck.

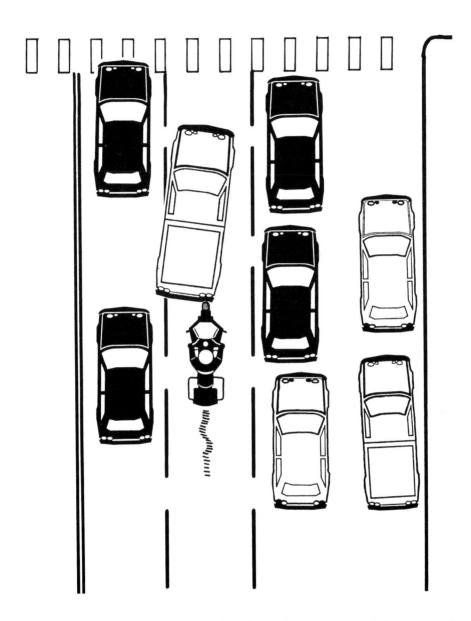

If you regularly practice your braking technique, you will be prepared to make quick stops in traffic. You can stop much quicker when using more front brake and less rear brake. The proper quick-stop technique is to squeeze the clutch and front brake simultaneously, squeezing the front brake progressively harder until the front tire is just short of a skid. Locking up the rear wheel may create noise and smoke, but it doesn't stop the bike very quickly. At the beginning of each riding season, it's smart to practice quick stops away from traffic to hone your braking skills.

One Clue to a Green Light About to Change Is the Pedestrian Signal

You're commuting home from work, shuffling along a busy four-lane arterial with a lot of lights. The stop-and-go traffic is frustrating, and the lights aren't synchronized. It's hard to judge when a light is going to turn red—you prefer not to run red lights if you can help it. But you don't want to be rear-ended if you stop too suddenly, nor do you want to get stuck in the intersection by slow traffic ahead.

Suddenly your concerns become reality. Just before you enter a crosswalk area, the green light changes to yellow. It's too late to stop, but before you can clear the intersection, traffic ahead slows to a crawl, the light turns red, and you are stranded in the intersection. Drivers beep their horns in annoyance, and you feel sheepish at being caught in such a stupid situation. It would also be easy to get nudged by angry drivers trying to squeeze around you.

It's important to make a "go" or "no-go" decision before you enter an intersection. One good clue to "stale" green lights is the Walk light for pedestrians. The pedestrian light always changes several seconds prior to the vehicle light to allow pedestrians time to get to the other curb. If you can see that the pedestrian Walk light is still on, it's a good bet the vehicle light will stay green for several more seconds. If the pedestrian light reads Don't Walk that's a good indication the vehicle signal is about to change, and you should plan to stop short of the intersection.

Taillight Trauma

It's Important to Ride Your Own Ride, Especially in Fast Company

You've been invited to go for a ride with some motorcyclists you met at the bike shop. You don't know these riders, but they all ride bikes similar to yours, are in the same age bracket, and wear quality riding gear. Showing up for the ride today, you look forward to socializing with them. You're a bit surprised when one of the leaders suddenly announces it's time to go, without any further explanation. You quickly get your helmet and gloves on but find yourself at the back of the pack as the leader accelerates down the street and turns off onto a narrow road into the hills.

The group turns out to be more aggressive than you had assumed, and you're concerned that the other riders will think you're less skilled than you are. To avoid falling behind, you simply focus on the taillight of the bike ahead and try to follow the same line at the same speed.

Suddenly, as you lean over hard into a tight corner, you feel your rear tire lose traction, and instinctively roll off the throttle, but that just makes it worse. The bike heads for the gravel shoulder, and you instantly know you're going to crash. Luckily, both you and the bike come to a stop in the underbrush without hitting any big rocks or trees. You aren't seriously injured, but you're very embarrassed, and your bike has extensive damage.

While it can be fun to ride with a group, you should understand that some riders are very competitive, and their group rides often turn out to be races—not social events. You should also be aware that riders at the back of a group must ride faster than the leader to catch up. It's easier to maintain your position if you are prepared to fall in directly behind the ride leader, rather than at the back of the pack.

Moreover, allowing yourself to focus on the taillight ahead will draw your attention away from riding your own bike. It's never smart to assume that you can maintain the same pace as a rider ahead simply by trying to do what he's doing. You are responsible for controlling your own bike, and that includes planning your own cornering lines for maximum traction, scrutinizing the surface for hazards, and making smooth throttle-to-brake transitions.

That Crack Sealant Snaking All Over the Road Is Slicker Than You Think

You're headed for the big motorcycle rally several states away. You rarely have time off to do much traveling by motorcycle, so on this trip you've been exploring the state highways and scenic roads as much as possible. Today, the weather is warm and dry. Traffic is sparse on the old highway you're following, and the curves are predictable, allowing you to enjoy an aggressive pace. You're curious but not concerned when you come upon a section of road covered in strange squiggles and lines. The lines appear to be some sort of sealant recently slathered over surface cracks in the asphalt.

Suddenly, as you're leaning into a sweeping right-hander, your rear tire steps sideways. Before you can do anything, the bike slams on its side, and instantly you're bouncing and sliding straight ahead, across the centerline. Fortunately, a car coming the other way sees your crash, and is able to stop without hitting you.

A lot of motorcyclists don't realize that some crack sealants are much more slippery than the surrounding asphalt, especially when fresh. If possible, you should avoid riding over such "tar snakes," especially when leaning into a turn. In this situation, the slippery tar was applied in wide strips all over the surface, which makes it impractical for you to avoid crossing them. When you observe such shiny-looking tar snakes ahead of you, reduce your speed to reduce your traction demands, the same as you would for a rain-slick road or for loose gravel.

Tentative Turners

Give Confused Drivers a Lot of Space

You're riding along a familiar four-lane urban arterial, approaching a major intersection with a left turn lane in the center, divided from the other traffic lanes by a solid white line. You have dropped back slightly from the car ahead, having noticed an out-of-state license plate and the nervous head turns of a driver who seems to be lost. When the driver enters the left turn lane, you are relieved to have him out of your way and accelerate toward the intersection to make the green light.

But before you get past the car, it suddenly swerves back across the white line, almost on top of you. You quickly roll off the gas, swerve toward the car on your right, and brake, barely squeezing yourself into a "white line" position inches between the two vehicles. The tentative turner gets through the intersection, but you are now stopped by a red light. You can barely control your rage at the illegal, arrogant, and stupid actions of a driver who doesn't seem to have even noticed you.

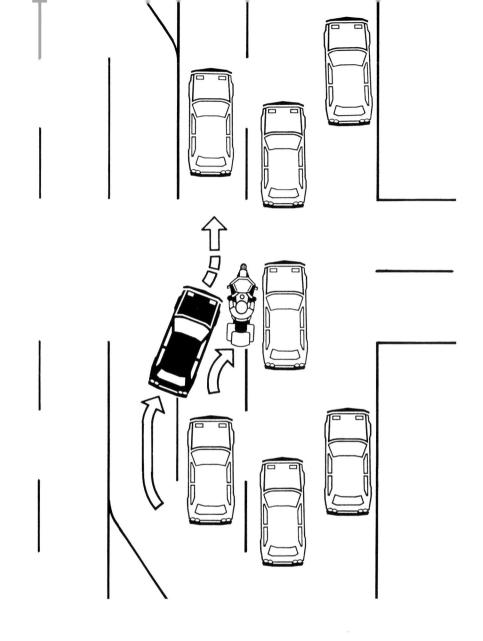

Yes, in this situation you do have the right-of-way, but you find yourself trying to avoid a collision that would certainly knock the bike down. Once you become aware of a driver who is apparently confused, you can separate yourself more from the vehicle, either by changing lanes, dropping farther back, or passing it before or after the intersection. In this case, such a confused driver may not see you at all or may assume that you are still behind him or her, even if you try to pass. And even without a tentative turner present, it isn't clever to accelerate toward a busy intersection.

In an Industrial Zone, Expect to Negotiate Some Serious Debris

You're on your way across town to meet some friends for a ride. You're running a little late, and it's been frustrating trying to make time through Saturday morning traffic. Now on a narrow two-lane road, there's a dump truck ahead, creeping along at 40 mph. Finally, you have had enough of being held up, and you decide to be more aggressive about passing. You ease over the centerline for a better view, then signal, accelerate up close behind the truck, and swing into the opposing lane for a quick pass.

But just as you attempt the pass, you realize a car is about to pull out of a driveway ahead, so you brake hard and pull back in line behind the truck. A couple of seconds later, the truck driver beeps his horn and swerves over toward the shoulder, exposing a large wooden timber lying in the road directly in your path. Your wheels are only a second from impact, so there's no time to take any evasive action. Instantly, your wheels slam into the timber, jolting the bike upward, and almost knocking the bars out of your grasp. As the bike bounces down on the other side of the timber, the steering goes mushy, and you're barely able to wobble the bike over onto the grassy shoulder without dropping it. Both of your wheel rims are bent, and both tires have deflated.

You should never be so focused on making time that you aren't watching for surface hazards. It's not uncommon to encounter loading timbers, wood blocks, and chain binders that have fallen off commercial trucks. By following so closely behind a truck, you severely limit your ability to take evasive action, even if the driver attempts to warn you by beeping.

In this situation, you should stay farther behind the truck to allow time to react to whatever problems might appear, including turning vehicles, pedestrians, and loose objects on the road. Your minimum following distance behind any vehicle should be two seconds. When you can't avoid following behind a large vehicle such as a truck or bus, consider increasing your following distance to four seconds.

Tire-Tread Terror

Slabs of Truck Tire Are a Major Concern

You've decided to spend the day at the races. It's early Sunday morning, the bike is packed with cold soda, snack food, and a fold-up camping chair. You've got a camera with a telephoto lens, sunscreen, and a pair of walking shoes so you don't have to trudge around all day in your riding boots. You're excited about getting out to the track, hyped up about high-performance motorcycling, and moving aggressively through freeway traffic.

There are more trucks on the road than you would have expected for a Sunday. You know that truckers have a limited view of what's around them, especially to the rear of a long trailer; therefore, you give them a lot of room and stay out of their blind spots. But just as you're about to pass a truck, it changes lanes in front of you to pass a slower vehicle, and you find yourself close behind. You notice the odor of burning rubber, hear a thumping sound, and notice that one of the trailer tires is bouncing up and down.

Before you can change lanes to get out from behind the truck, you hear a sudden, hollow *whump*, and a large piece of something is flying through the air, bouncing and tumbling in your direction. You swerve left in an attempt to miss it, but it slams into the front of your fairing, brushes your boot, and smashes against the rear of the bike. You're barely able to get the bike in control and bring it to a stop on the shoulder without dropping it. Your front fender is shattered, the lower fairing is in tatters, and your right saddlebag's missing. Looking back, you see the culprit: a huge section of truck tire tread. By now, the truck has disappeared, your gear has been pulverized in traffic, and you're on your own to limp your bike home.

It's hazardous to ride near trucks, but sometimes it's unavoidable. If you observe a slower-moving vehicle up ahead in the right lane in front of a truck, you can predict that the truck will change lanes into your lane to pass it. If this happens, you can back off or change lanes to get out of its way. You don't want to follow it too closely because truck-tread separation is a common hazard on fast highways, and even a small section of tread can cause severe damage or injury to a motorcyclist. If you smell and hear the symptoms of a failing tire, you should immediately take evasive action to get even farther away.

If Your Bike Makes Sparks in the Corners, Is It the Bike or Your Technique?

You enjoy cruising the freeways on your big touring machine, but sometimes it's nice to get off the superslab and explore the secondary highways and country lanes. Usually you just motor along at a sedate pace on scenic roads, but today you're riding with some friends who seem to want to ride more aggressively, and you don't want them to think you aren't a skilled rider.

Although your bike is the same model as theirs, yours seems to scrape more as you try to keep up, and that makes you nervous. It also doesn't seem able to corner as fast as your friends' bikes. You try to make up for the problem by riding faster in the straights and then rolling off the throttle and braking as you enter the next curve, but your companions still leave you in their dust.

As you enter one very tight turn, you feel it necessary to ride the rear brake as you lean the bike, but this time something under the bike touches down with a horrible scrape, and it feels as if the bike is going to lever itself off the tires. To avoid a slideout, you release the brakes and steer the machine wider, across the centerline.

Part of the problem may be your machine. If you add heavy loads or a lot of accessories to your motorcycle, increase the suspension preloads to keep the motorcycle in the middle of its suspension travel and keep your tires pumped up to recommended pressures. It's also important that any added accessories such as engine guards don't decrease leanover clearance.

Whatever the machine, better cornering tactics should help you keep up with your buddies. Enter corners from the outside of your lane and select a line with the most gradual curve to conserve traction and minimize lean. Get your braking done before you lean over. Slow to a corner-entry speed that allows you to ease on the throttle all the way through the rest of the curve. Rolling on some throttle as you lean the bike maximizes traction and maintains leanover clearance.

Traction Trouble

Watch Traction in Patches of Loose Sand and Gravel

It's been a good day for exploring the country. The bike has been running great, and the weather is just right. You're not in a hurry today, so you just putter along in the center of the lane. You know that there are few traffics signs and signals, and that local drivers often ignore them. So, when you notice the Cross-Traffic Does Not Stop note under the Stop sign, you prepare for a complete stop well before the white line.

But as you squeeze on the front brake, your front tire suddenly loses traction and slides out. Before you even realize what's happening, the bike slams over on its side, dumping you in an embarrassing heap in the middle of the road. As you attempt to pick up the bike, you realize that much of the asphalt surface at this intersection is covered in fine loose gravel.

While you always need to observe the street signs, you also need to constantly monitor the road surface. Those double yellow centerlines may not be faded paint; they could be covered by a layer of loose material. Changes in color or texture of the road surface are important clues that traction will probably change too. If you observe rougher-looking areas on the surface or realize that a lighter color is some loose gravel, you can brake earlier and more gently. You also can position your wheels in areas where car tires have pushed the gravel aside. When braking in low-traction situations, it helps to squeeze the clutch before braking and to use both front and rear brakes simultaneously.

Trespassing Turners

Leave a Little Extra Space for Drivers Who Cut Corners

You're returning home from a quick trip to the motorcycle dealer where you picked up some oil filters. Traffic is always fast and furious on Saturdays, so you're watching carefully for left-turning cars at intersections, especially on this busy urban arterial.

Your route home requires you to make a left turn, but you know that it isn't smart to stop in an unprotected traffic lane where you could easily be struck from behind by an inattentive driver. Fortunately, you know of a cross street with a left turn lane controlled by a traffic signal. Here you can make a safer turn. You activate your right turn signal and pull into the left turn lane. A white truck on your right is wandering over the white line, so you move left as you pass by, and watch the driver carefully.

Suddenly, before you reach the end of the lane, a left-turning car shoots from the cross street and cuts around you. You're surprised, but manage to do a quick stop a few inches short of a collision. You're incensed that a left-turning driver cut the corner and almost hit you.

Even if you make a turn at a controlled intersection and are wary of other vehicles (such as that wandering truck), you should maintain your awareness of the entire situation, predicting that a left-turner might emerge from your right. Be aware that car drivers often cut corners when turning, so always plan your stops a few feet short of the end of the lane to provide a space cushion. In this case, had you already been stopped at the outside corner of the left turn lane when the car made its turn, you would have been hit.

Tricky Tracks

Streetcar Tracks Need a Clever Plan of Attack

You're cruising around a seaside town on a Sunday afternoon, looking for a place to eat. Streetcar tracks run down the middle of a one-way street, but you haven't seen any streetcars in use. Traffic is light. There aren't even many pedestrians. For once you can relax and just enjoy the area.

When you see a Stop Ahead sign painted on the surface, you prepare to make a full stop short of the crosswalk, just in case a pedestrian steps out from behind a parked car. You notice that the streetcar tracks angle across the street, but you're not concerned about colliding with a streetcar.

Suddenly, before you can bring the bike to a stop, the front wheel seems to dart off to the right, and the bike tilts left. You quickly release the front brake and attempt to countersteer to keep the bike balanced, but it doesn't seem to respond. Before you can do anything, the bike crashes over onto its side in the middle of the street.

Driving on a street with streetcar tracks is trickier than it seems. The hazard isn't a streetcar coming—it's the rails crossing in close proximity and at a slight angle to where you must stop. Never brake when your tires are crossing shiny surfaces in the street, especially railroad or streetcar tracks. In this particular situation (see photo), you can move over to the far right side of the lane and bring the bike to a stop, then turn the bike to cross the rails at a greater angle. Or, since this is a one-way street, move left and cross the rails earlier and then make your stop on the left side of the street.

Remember that in order to balance a two-wheeler, you require front-wheel traction. If you are braking when your front tire crosses the shiny steel rails of a streetcar track, your front wheel will momentarily lock up and slide sideways. Countersteering won't have any effect because the tire doesn't have enough traction to force the contact patch back under the center of gravity.

You're Only Paranoid If They Aren't Out to Get You

You're riding along a six-lane urban arterial with a full-length left turn lane in the center. Your plan is to make a left turn into a shopping mall. Approaching the mall, you signal, pull into the left turn lane, and shift down to prepare for the turn. You scrutinize the street for oncoming traffic, the mall exit for anyone who might pull out onto the street, and for pedestrians crossing the mall entrance. Oncoming traffic is adequately distant, and there are no pedestrians nearby, but there is a pickup truck in a position to pull out of the mall exit. Eye contact with the driver confirms that she sees you, so you continue your left turn into the parking lot, rolling on a little throttle as you lean the bike.

Suddenly, the pickup truck shoots into the street, making a left turn directly into your path. You quickly hit the brakes, and with both tires sliding, you manage to bring the bike to a stop inches short of a collision. The other driver speeds away. Even though you were smart to watch for other users, to signal your intentions early, and to prepare for the turn by shifting to a lower gear, apparently you were fooled into thinking that because you had eye contact with a driver, that driver would stay out of your way.

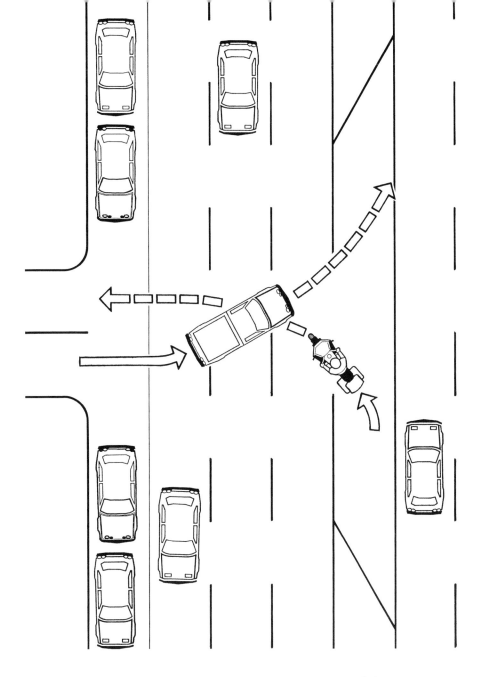

To avoid a collision, you must maintain awareness of the movement of other vehicles and be prepared to get out of their way. Rather than trying to establish eye contact with a driver, it's more important to watch the top of the other vehicle's front tire to get the first hint of movement. Whenever you approach a suspicious situation, you should be lightly applying the front brake to prepare for a quick stop. If you're already on the brake, it's more likely you'll be able to stop quickly without losing control, even in a turn.

Wet Bricks

Bricks Are Made Out of Clay That Gets Slippery When Wet

You're riding a side street in the old part of town after a brief rain. There are many parked cars that might suddenly pull out of parking spaces, and intersections where cars might turn in front of you, so you scan the other vehicles for movement. And because the street surface is still wet and you know wet pavement has reduced traction, you increase your following distance. But where the bricked street curves to the left, you suddenly feel the front tire wiggle. You panic, instinctively roll off the throttle, and attempt to steer the bike toward the curve. Before you can regain balance, the bike crashes on its left side.

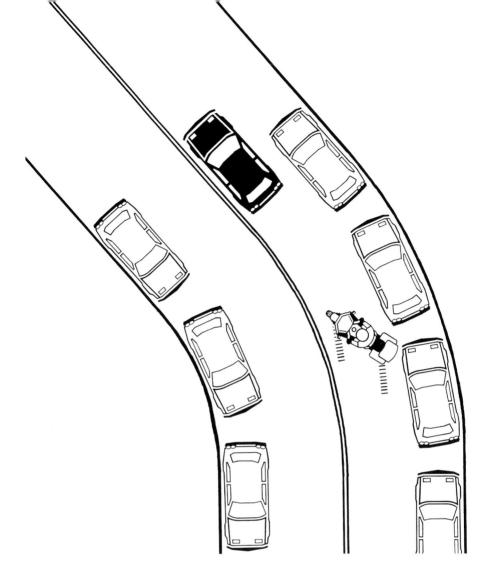

When the pavement is wet, you not only need to scrutinize the other vehicles around you to avoid collisions and to increase following distance, but you must also observe the street surface. Brick paving has acceptable traction when dry, but wet bricks are often treacherous. The clay particles worn loose by traffic mix with water to form a thin film of slippery clay. Wet-brick surfaces are slickest after a brief shower, before there has been enough water to wash away the clay.

In this situation, you should observe the wet bricks, realize the bricks are probably more slippery than the surrounding pavement, and manage traction more effectively. Remember that rolling off the throttle applies engine braking to the rear wheel, which can contribute to a slideout. Reducing speed before the curve, following a straighter line through the curve to keep the bike more vertical, and holding a steady throttle all help conserve traction and prevent a slideout.

White Curbs

Think of Solid White Lines As Curbs— Many of Them Are

It's a warm Saturday evening, and you've decided to go for a ride. You understand the importance of being visible at night, so you have checked your lights and are wearing your riding jacket with reflective stripes. You turn onto the freeway entrance, accelerate up to traffic speed, and signal for a lane change to merge with traffic. You scan your mirrors to ensure the other lane is clear, and begin to ease across the solid white line.

But just as your tires reach the white line, the handlebars are wrenched from your grasp. You fight for control, but the motorcycle seems to trip and fall. Shocked, you find yourself sliding down the pavement, your motorcycle grinding a trail of sparks ahead of you. Fortunately, the drivers behind you see your reflective jacket, and stop to protect you from getting run over.

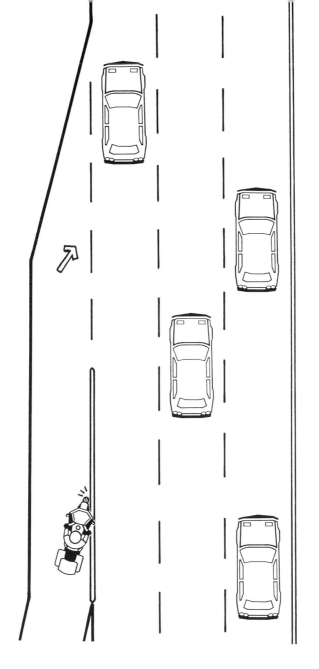

Sometimes the white lines near merging lanes are actually painted on a concrete lane divider, similar to a low curb. When merging, delay your lane change until you reach the dashed white lines indicating the correct location to merge (especially at night, when it is harder to see the distinction). Before crossing a solid white line, a motorcyclist should always scrutinize the road surface for curbs or grooves that might trap the tires. The reason for the crash in this scenario is that the front tire eased up to the divider but couldn't jump over it, so the front wheel couldn't be countersteered to maintain balance.

Wibble-Wobbles

Maybe You've Got a Bike Problem— or Maybe Your Skills Need Work

When you got into motorcycling a couple of years ago, you bought a used bike. At first, when you were just learning how to handle it, you took it easy, especially on twisty roads. But now that you've gained more riding experience, you're beginning to ride a little more aggressively, and you've begun to notice that your machine has some strange behavior, especially if you try to push it a little fast through corners. You find it unnerving when the bike sort of wibble-wobbles in the middle of the turn. It's as if the bike can't decide which line to follow or whether to lean over more or straighten up. Is there something wrong with your bike?

It's good to pay attention to your machine's strange movements because it's trying to tell you something. It's possible your bike has a problem, such as worn swing arm bearings or shock absorbers that are overdue for replacement. It's also important to inflate your tires to correct pressures for the load.

But it's just as likely that your cornering technique is a culprit. Consider how you use the throttle. If you lean the bike into a turn on a trailing throttle or ride the rear brake deep into a turn, it's almost impossible to avoid a wobble at the point where you get off the brakes and back on the gas. The bike will be more stable and predictable when you decelerate in a straight line *before* you lean over, then gradually ease on more throttle as you lean the bike into the turn. Rolling on the throttle while leaning over helps stabilize speed and suspension, which lets the machine follow a smoother line without those wibble-wobbles.

Windy-Wambles

The Only Way to Get the Bike Leaned Upwind Quickly Is to Countersteer

You've been itching for a long ride ever since the weather warmed up, and this weekend you decide that motorcycling will have top priority, even though the forecast is calling for gusting winds. You top up the engine oil, pump up the tires to correct pressure, check that all the lights are working, pack your rain gear, wiggle in your earplugs, and suit up for a serious ride.

Leaving town in Saturday morning traffic, you make a point of staying out of the blind spots of other drivers, watching for potential left-turners, covering the front brake lever, and avoiding surface hazards such as the dribbles of oil that collect in the center of the lane just before traffic signals. You intend to have a long, hard ride, not spend the day filling out accident forms.

But gusty winds are picking up, and later that afternoon as you're halfway across a high bridge, a sudden wind gust from your right slams into the bike and pushes it left toward the centerline. You attempt to lean the bike upwind by shifting your weight, but you can't get it leaned quickly enough to avoid drifting over the centerline into the opposing lane. Fortunately, the driver of an oncoming car swerves out of your way to avoid a head-on collision, and as the gust abates, you are finally able to get the bike back into the right lane. At the end of the bridge, you pull over to relax.

In situations such as a sudden wind gust from your right, you must use countersteering (not just thinking *lean* and shifting your weight to get the bike leaned quickly) to keep the bike straight. Pushing hard on the right grip will force the bike to lean upwind. Then, as the gust passes, pushing on the left grip causes the bike to straighten up. To prepare yourself for quick changes of lean angle, practice countersteering as the primary way you control balance and direction.

Wood Surfaces Can Be Surprisingly Slick When Wet

The weather has been sunny and warm, and it's been a great ride out in the country. The old highway curves through farmland, crossing and re-crossing a nearby railroad track as it snakes down the valley. Some of the crossings are with the highway snaking beneath a high wooden trestle, others with a wooden bridge curving over the track. It's been fun playing tag with the railroad track, but with rain clouds moving in you have decided to head for home.

On your way back, the fresh rain is dampening the pavement, so you ride a little less aggressively. Approaching one of the bridges crossing over the railroad tracks, you realize the wooden deck is curved, but the curve isn't any sharper than the other curves in the road. But as your tires roll onto the wooden surface, you feel the bike wiggle. The wet wood feels as slippery as ice. You wisely hold a steady throttle, keep the bike upright, stay off the brakes, and apply the lightest possible steering pressure on the grips. You are amazed at how slippery the wooden deck got with just a sprinkle of rain, and you now approach the other bridges even more cautiously.

It's wise to ride more cautiously during a fresh rainfall, and the tactics in this scenario are correct for maintaining balance on a slick surface. But wooden surfaces can be extremely slippery when wet, so you should approach a wet, curving wooden bridge even more conservatively. Wood fibers get ground away by the abrasion of passing traffic, and these loose fibers mix with rainwater to form a slippery paste. Some of the slippery wood paste will wash away during a heavy rainfall, so you should assume that wooden decks will be most hazardous during the first few minutes of a new rain or when they are damp from dew.

Work-Zone Woes

Construction Zones Demand Special Riding Tactics

Now that you've discovered how practical it is to commute to work by bike, you've been riding to work most of the year. Of course, commuting requires that you be wary of other drivers, watch for surface hazards, and always carry rain gear. You know that some drivers are only half-awake, and others are hurrying to make it to work on time, so you're prepared to get out of their way. This morning you are relieved that commuter traffic isn't as aggressive as usual.

Approaching an odd, five-way intersection, you observe loose gravel on the surface and a car coming the other way that could turn left down a side street. You predict the other driver might turn in front of you, and the loose gravel will make stopping difficult. You quickly decelerate, shift down, apply the front brake lightly, and prepare for a quick stop before you reach the loose gravel. When the oncoming car doesn't turn, you ease off the brake and roll on the throttle to get back up to speed.

But suddenly the rear of the bike slides right and then fishtails back to the left. Your survival instinct is to snap the throttle closed and jam on the rear brake, but months of commuting have taught you to avoid doing anything suddenly when there is a traction problem. Instead, you gradually ease off the throttle, and the bike recovers. As the bike thumps over the second steel construction plate, you realize that attempting to accelerate while crossing the shiny steel caused the rear tire to slide out.

In the morning, you can expect steel construction plates to be slick with morning dew and oil drips. Even with many other surface hazards and aggressive traffic present you need to take the time to cross construction plates with caution. With the engine in a lower gear, you should maintain a steady speed and avoid accelerating until you have crossed all the steel plates.

LIST OF ABBREVIATIONS

ABS: antilock braking system

BEMC: Boeing Employees' Motorcycle Club

MCN: *Motorcycle Consumer News*

mph: miles per hour

MSF: Motorcycle Safety Foundation

SUV: Sport Utility Vehicle

ABOUT THE AUTHOR

David L. Hough is a longtime motorcyclist and journalist. The Flemish name "Hough" is pronounced like "rough" or "tough." Dave and his wife, Diana, currently reside near Port Angeles, Washington, about 70 miles northwest of Seattle. The Houghs have traveled extensively throughout the United States, Canada, Great Britain, Ireland, Germany, Switzerland, Austria, and South Africa, on both two-wheeled and three-wheeled motorcycles.

Dave's daily commutes by motorcycle through city traffic for twenty-five years provided an ongoing stream of real-life experiences that stimulated ideas for skill articles. His writings, photographs, and illustrations have appeared in various motorcycle publications. Special awards from the Motorcycle Safety Foundation have recognized him for his riding skill articles in *Road Rider* and *Motorcycle Consumer News*.

Dave earned his instructor certification from the Motorcycle Safety Foundation (MSF) in 1981, and is also a chief instructor for the Sidecar/Trike Education Program. Many of his ideas on rider training have been incorporated into the MSF "Experienced RiderCourse," and the S/TEP three-wheeler courses. He selected "Proficient Motorcycling" columns from *Motorcycle Consumer News* for his book, *Proficient Motorcycling*, which was published by BowTie™ Press in 2000. He is an accomplished illustrator, photographer, carpenter, mechanic, plumber, electrician, welder, boat builder, tour director, and grandparent.

For more information on motorcycling, check out the *Motorcycle Consumer News* Web site at www.mcnews.com. *MCN* accepts no commercial advertising and is wholly supported by its readers. Since there are no industry influences on reporting, *MCN* has the best in-depth evaluations, product comparisons, and technical features.

Check out *Proficient Motorcycling,* also by David L. Hough, for more information on safe motorcycling. Culled from the famous series of articles of the same name, David teaches you how to develop your riding skills and avoid pitfalls so you can make it to the end of your ride in one piece and still have fun.